The Economist in Business

Editors

K. J. W. ALEXANDER
A. G. KEMP
T. M. RYBCZYNSKI

REPRINTS OF ECONOMIC CLASSICS

Augustus M. Kelley · Publishers
NEW YORK 1969

Published in the U. S. A. by
AUGUSTUS M. KELLEY, PUBLISHERS
New York, New York

Printed in Great Britain by
Western Printing Services Ltd., Bristol

The Economist in Business

Editors
K. J. W. ALEXANDER, A. G. KEMP,
T. M. RYBCZYNSKI

Contents

Preface

by THE EDITORS

This collection of essays on the role of economists in British industry has developed from the interest aroused within the
Business Economists' Group by the Survey which is published
as the first essay in this book. The survey arose from a happy
coincidence of interests between the Business Economists' Group
which required information about the employment of its members and one of the editors, who was in process of establishing a
Department of Economics in a new university and felt that some
'market research' on how graduate economists were used in
industry would be helpful in the construction of courses.

As the survey proceeded it became obvious that much of the
interesting detail relating to the work of economists in industry
could only be provided in depth by inviting lengthy contributions from individual practitioners. This has been done, and
now provides the first detailed pictures of the whole range of
employments and highlights the current problems of an emer-
gent profession. Some of these problems are singled out for
special mention in the last essay which deals with 'The Future
of the Profession'.

The Editors wish to thank members of the Business Economists' Group and many other economists in business whose
co-operation has been necessary for the production of this book.
Thanks are also due to the many firms which have provided information. The Editors wish to put on record their indebtedness
to Mrs. C. Sandell for administrative and secretarial help.

1

The Economist in Business: A Survey

by K. J. W. ALEXANDER *and* ALEXANDER G. KEMP

I. Background

This survey has been undertaken by the authors in conjunction with the Business Economists' Group. Its purposes are broadly to analyse (1) how the economist is employed by businesses and public services in Britain to-day, (2) the business economist's actual functions, (3) the relevance of his qualifications and training for his present functions, (4) how efficiently his expertise is utilised, (5) his remuneration and conditions of service, and (6) his career prospects. A further analysis of the present state of the market for economists has also been made, and in addition the views of senior management on the employment of economists in their organisations have been sought but are dealt with elsewhere. The study is considered opportune because (1) the profession is a relatively young one about which little is known, (2) the profession is an expanding one, (3) the current rapid expansion in the economics faculties in British universities is creating both problems and opportunities. It is hoped that useful information for business economists, business leaders in the U.K., and academic economists will be gained as a result of this Report.

The survey originated at the request of the Business Economists' Group (B.E.G.) which wanted to have a general analysis of the activities of its members. So far as academic economists are concerned interest in the development of the profession of the business economist is primarily due to a desire to discover (1) to what extent the economics taught at university is relevant to the problems tackled by business economists, (2) what additional economic techniques have had to be acquired by business economists after graduation, and (3) how efficiently economists are employed in industry.

Method

The survey has been conducted mainly by postal questionnaires. The main questionnaire (comprising 24 pages and 72 questions) was sent to all non-academic members of the B.E.G., colleagues and business economist friends nominated by members, respondents to letters in *The Economist, The Statist* and the *Economic Journal* regarding the survey, and to economist members of the Industrial Market Research Association. In addition discussions were held with several business economists. A further postal questionnaire surveyed all firms and other non-academic organisations who advertised for economists in *The Economist* between January and June 1965. An analysis was also made of all advertisements for economists in *The Economist* since 1945. Top management and 'users' of business economists in various types of industries and organisations were interviewed and asked to complete a questionnaire.* The main questionnaire was sent out at Easter 1965, and so information regarding the 'present position' should be taken as referring to mid-1965. The questions were both factual and qualitative, but as far as possible questions were put in a form suitable for data processing. The response rates are as shown in Table 1.

TABLE 1. Response Rates to Questionnaire

	B.E.G. members	Friends of B.E.G. members	Press advertisements	Economist members of IMRA	Total
No. invited	335	57	33	57	482
No. of respondents	227	33	23	23	306
Per cent response	68	58	70	58	63

It cannot, of course, be claimed that the sample is a representative one. Thus a main part of the sample consists of

* Considerably more data was collected in these various ways than has been used in this Report. Certain additional information can be provided to readers, who should communicate with one of the authors.

members of the Business Economists' Group. This seems to be a
major reason for the rather unexpected age distribution of the
sample (see Table 3). Members of the Business Economists'
Group tend not to come predominantly from the younger age
groups. It is interesting to note, however, that the age distribution of the sample is not markedly different from that found in
the Committee on the National Science Foundation Report on
the Economics Profession entitled *The Structure of Economists'
Employment and Salaries, 1964* (*American Economic Review* Supple-
ment, Part 2, December 1965).

II. General Introductory Information on Respondents

(a) Broad Qualifications

Of the 306 respondents 293 possessed a university degree and
260 'majored' in economics. The distribution of the class of
degree held is indicated in Table 2.

TABLE 2. Distribution of Class of Degree—all Respondents

	First	Second (upper division)	Second (lower division)	Second un-specified	Third	Other
Per cent of total	9	42	27	10	6	5

In addition 52 graduates (18 per cent) had undertaken a post-
graduate course and in some cases a post-graduate degree.

(b) Age

As is to be expected in a young and rapidly growing profession
the age structure of the respondents is a relatively young one.
The distribution is shown in Table 3.

TABLE 3. Age Structure of Business Economists

Years	No.	Years	No.
20–22	4	36–40	48
23–25	25	41–45	33
26–28	34	46–50	19
29–31	48	51–59	13
32–35	77	60+	1

From Table 3 it can be seen that 62 per cent of all respondents were in the age group 20–35 years. There are important implications of this age distribution, particularly regarding mobility which is considered in more detail below. However, the main point is simply that the relatively young age structure is likely to permit an unusually high degree of mobility. Further, the fact that there are relatively few business economists with very long experience may well mean that, *caeteris paribus*, business economists can expect to attain positions of greater responsibility at a relatively earlier age than people in other professions. This is all the more likely because of another factor, namely that many business economists expect not to remain as pure economists throughout their career, but to enter general management. This is discussed in detail below in Section VIII.

III. Organisation

One way of classifying business economists is by type of employer. For respondents the result by broad category is as follows:

TABLE 4. Type of Employer of Business Economists

Type	Number
Industrial	181
Commercial and Financial	61
Governmental and Public	23
No information	41
	306

Thus 68 per cent of respondents who gave information were employed by industrial firms, 23 per cent by commercial/financial establishments and 9 per cent by Government/public bodies. As the figures relate to 1965 they are probably a fair reflection of the present broad pattern of employment of business economists. The recent upsurge in employment of economists by the Government has meant that the share of the Government/public bodies sector as an employer of business economists has increased in the last year or so. Nevertheless the demand for economists by all sectors is increasing and is expected to increase (see Section VIII where there is also mention of what the broad pattern of type of employer is likely to be in the future).

The industrial employers of economists can be analysed further in terms of size by turnover and number of employees. The results are shown in Tables 5 and 6.

Turnover £m	No. of respondents	Numbers employed	No. of respondents
Under 10	26	Under 2,000	35
11– 30	24	2,001– 4,000	14
31– 60	22	4,001– 6,000	10
61– 100	16	6,001– 8,000	14
101– 300	27	8,001– 10,000	7
301– 500	12	10,001– 15,000	18
501– 750	7	15,001– 25,000	23
751–1,000	—	25,001– 50,000	14
1,001–3,000	18	50,001–100,000	22
Over 3,000	—	Over 100,000	—
No information	29	No information	24
TOTAL	181	TOTAL	181

TABLE 5. / TABLE 6.

Taking turnover first as indicating the size of firms it can be seen that the spread of employment of economists is fairly wide. This is to be expected as it reflects the facts that (a) there are a smaller number of relatively large firms than relatively small firms in the employing sector and (b) that larger firms will tend to employ more economists than smaller firms. These factors which operate in opposing directions help to explain the wide spread of employment. When numbers employed is taken as the criterion of size the pattern is rather different, but still exhibits a wide spread of employment. About 50 per cent are employed in firms with over 10,000 employees, but yet about 24 per cent are employed in firms with less than 2,000 employees. This diversity again reflects the two opposing factors mentioned above.

The mobility of economists is a question which has been given much publicity recently. There is a difficulty in arriving at a criterion for evaluating the mobility of business economists, particularly as there are no comparable figures for other professions. The statistics from respondents to questions on mobility indicate rather surprisingly that 41 per cent of business economists have been employed by only one organisation, and that another 33 per cent have been employed by only two organisations, (statistics refer to all employing sectors). This is rather unexpected when the present great scarcity of business economists is considered. The influence of the relative youth of the profession is rather difficult to assess. It is likely that younger people are inclined to be more mobile, but on the other hand they have not had the same time to effect this inclination. A further more detailed analysis of the mobility of business economists is shown in Table 7.

TABLE 7.

No. of years with	First firm employed with	Second firm employed with	Third firm employed with	Fourth firm employed with	Fifth firm employed with	Sixth firm employed with
0– 2	140	118	69	34	17	5
3– 5	86	77	57	30	11	4
6– 9	30	28	19	10	5	
10–15	24	12	7	8		1
16 and over	20	2	6	1		
TOTAL	300	237	158	83	33	10
No information	6	69	148	223	273	296

(Two of the 306 economists had more than six employers—one had nine and the other ten.)

This table relates the number of years worked by the economists to the number of separate firms/organisations by which they have been employed. The result reflects (a) the fact (noted above) that a large proportion of business economists have stayed with their original employer for a long time, and (b) that when business economists have changed their employment they have tended to leave their original employer within a fairly short period. It must be stressed that these deductions can only be made in a fairly loose way because, of course, the *age pattern* of the economists is also a variable affecting the pattern of mobility.

The relationship between age and mobility is shown in Table 8.

TABLE 8. Age and Number of Firms Worked for.

Age	Number of firms worked for							
	One	Two	Three	Four	Five	Six	Blank	Total
Blank	1						1	2
20–22	3	1						4
23–25	16	6					3	25
26–28	13	15	5				1	34
29–31	23	9	9	4			3	48
32–35	19	29	14	6	1		8	77
36–40	12	14	9	6	3	1	3	48
41–45	13	6	7		2	1	4	33
46–50	6	7	2		2	1	1	19
51–59	6	3	2				2	13
60+	2	1						3
TOTAL	114	91	48	16	8	3	26	306

From Table 8 it can be seen that there is only a slight tendency for mobility of economists to increase with their age. This is probably again due to the two opposing factors at work—namely that younger people are likely to be 'naturally' more mobility-inclined than older, but they have had less time to put this tendency into practice.

The distribution of employment of business economists by numbers per firm is indicated in Table 9.

Table 9 suggests that in the U.K. about 55 per cent of organisations which employ economists have four or less and 74 per cent have nine or less. How this position has been changing and is likely to change in future is discussed in Section VIII. Table 10 shows the distribution of economists who are located in separate Economics Departments of their organisations. It is significant that about 59 per cent of respondents are *not* employed in a separate Economics Department. Furthermore of those who are employed in a separate department 71 per cent are in departments of nine members and under. These statistics underline the point that the profession is still at an embryo stage.

It is pertinent to consider to which departments those

economists not employed in separate Economics Departments are attached. This is indicated in Table 11.

TABLE 9. Distribution of Economists by firms.

No. of Economists	No. of Firms
1– 4	141
5– 9	47
10–14	12
15–19	15
20–24	4
25–29	7
30–39	4
40–49	6
50–59	1
60–69	10
70–99	2
100 and over	4
	253

TABLE 10. Economists in Separate Economics Departments

No. of Economists	No. of Respondents in Separate Economics Departments
1– 4	49
5– 9	39
10–14	10
15–19	5
20–24	4
25 and over	17
	124

TABLE 11. Location of Economists not in Separate Economics Departments

Department	Number	Department	Number
Market Research	54	Planning	29
Marketing	44	Investment	12
Distribution	3	Finance	7
Supply	6	Production	2
Others	65		

Though some of these departments—e.g. Planning—will have rather different meanings in different firms the main point is clear, that a very large proportion of these economists is attached to Marketing departments. This emphasis on marketing activities remains when the question of the working relationships between Economics Departments and other departments is considered. This is illustrated in Table 12 where the influence of Marketing Departments is seen to be still pronounced.

TABLE 12. Working Relationships between
Economics and Other Departments (figures show percentage of total number of Economics Depts.)

	Close Co-operation	Some Liason
Marketing	18	15
Market Research	16	11
Distribution	6	9
Planning	16	10
Finance	14	12
Investment	12	11
Production	6	18
Supply	5	10
Other	7	4

Reporting and Work Initiation Relationships

There is obviously a logical connection between reporting relationships of individuals in an organisation and their departmental location. This is borne out in the case of business economists. The Head of the Department concerned reported direct to the Board of Directors in 45 per cent of cases. In 9 per cent of cases the Head of the Department reported to the Marketing Manager. This was in fact easily the second most important relationship, there being no other single relationship of great significance. From the point of view of the business economist it seems encouraging that in 73 per cent of cases the Head of his department does have access to the Board of Directors.

A question related to the reporting relationships is that of the initiation of work. The Board of Directors is again found to be a significant source. This is illustrated in Table 13.

It is clear from this table that there is wide variety in the

B

TABLE 13. Proportion of Work of
Business Economists Initiated by Board of Directors

Work Initiated by Board	Proportion of Respondents
%	%
0– 9	20
10– 19	16
20– 29	17
30– 49	16
50– 74	19
75–100	12

proportion of the work of economists initiated by the Board. This is to be expected for several reasons: (a) the great variation in the size of companies; clearly the larger the size of the company the greater the ability to delegate responsibilities, (b) the *type* of employing organisation. Thus in a firm of economic consultants where the economist is central to the operation of the company's business the Board is likely to initiate his work, but in a large industrial organisation with a small service Economics Department the Board may well not initiate much if any of the economist's work, (c) finally, and closely related to (b), the *function* of the economist in the organisation. It is to be expected that the more operational the nature of the economist's work the greater is the likelihood that a substantial part of his work will be initiated by the Board. Clearly there can be no general rule stating baldly how much of any business economist's work should be initiated by the Board.

On examination it was found that a higher proportion of the work of industrial firms was initiated by the Board of Directors compared to commercial and financial firms and public bodies. With industrial firms it was also found that there was a slight inverse relationship between the size of firm and the proportion initiated by the Board. This is to be expected in view of the greater opportunities for delegation in the larger firms. Since economists often work in a specialist advisory capacity (see Section IV), and since in such capacities it was thought that considerable individual initiative might have to be taken, an attempt was made to determine how far this might be true. The results are summarised in Table 14.

TABLE 14.

Proportion of Work of Economists Initiated by Themselves
and by Economics Department

Proportion of Work %	Initiated by:	
	Individual Economist % of total	Economics Dept. % of total
0– 9	23	24
10– 19	23	22
20– 29	18	13
30– 49	18	21
50– 74	9	12
75–100	9	8

There is again a fairly wide spread of work initiation which is to
be expected when the relevant variables are considered. Factors
mentioned in the previous few paragraphs such as type and size
of the organisation, and the functions of the economist/Econo-
mics Department are clearly operative, and as they are probably
not operating in the same direction they will tend to make the
distribution a fairly widely-spread one. Another factor, namely
the degree of seniority of the economist concerned will also be
relevant. It is to be expected, *caeteris paribus*, that the more
senior the position of the economist the more scope he will have
for initiating work on his own accord.

IV. Functions of the Business Economist

The functions of the business economist can be classified in many
different ways. It is useful to start the analysis by looking at his
job categorised under fairly broad headings. One such classification is shown in Table 15.

A more illuminating relationship would at first sight appear to
be that between the age of business economists and the nature
of their job. This is shown in Table 16. In fact the relationship
is seen to be not very pronounced. This probably reflects the fact
that different organisations employ their economists in different
ways functionally, and that age as such is not, in general, a
major determining factor. It is more likely that in any *one* firm
the influence of age is determining the nature of job may be
more pronounced.

When the nature of the economist's job (as classified above) was related to type of employer it was found that the commercial/financial sector had the highest analytical content. Little relationship could be discerned, however, between size of employer and nature of job.

TABLE 15. Nature of Job of Business Economists

Informational Nature	Analytical Nature	Percentage of Respondents
Per cent of working time	Per cent	
0	100	9
20	80	52
60	40	30
80	20	9
0	100	—

TABLE 16. Age of Business Economist and Nature of Job.

Inf./ Analytical Per cent	Blank	20–22	23–25	26–28	29–31	32–35	36–40	41–45	46–50	51–59	60+	TOTAL
0–100		1	2	2	3	5	10	1		1		25
20– 80	2	2	13	14	24	40	18	16	11	6		146
60– 40		1	5	13	17	17	12	8	7	2	2	84
80 –20 100– 0			4	4	1	8	1	3		4	1	26
Blank			1	1	3	7	7	5	1			25
TOTAL	2	4	25	34	48	77	48	33	19	13	3	306

The functions of the economist can be broadly classified in another way. This is shown in Table 17.

TABLE 17. Nature of Work of Individual Economist.

Nature of Work	Per cent of Respondents
Provide a general economic intelligence service	10
Provide a specialist service	30
Provide both	60

The main conclusion which can be drawn from this is that specialisation of work has not proceeded very far among business economists in the U.K. This is very understandable in the light of the earlier conclusions regarding the fairly small size of the average economics department and the fact that 59 per cent of business economists were not located in separate economics departments at all. The main point is further illustrated when the extent to which departments sub-divide on specialist lines is considered, as in Table 18.

TABLE 18. Sectional Specialisation of Departments

	No. of Respondents	Per cent
Departments with specialist sections	87	35
Departments with no specialist sections	166	65

The question of the degree of specialisation in the business economist's work can be looked at in other ways and one such is indicated in Table 19.

TABLE 19. Time of Economist Spent in Different Functions

Per cent of Working Time	Operational Work	Fore-casting	Economic Information	Statistical Analysis	Other
	(Number of Respondents)				
0– 19	46	98	76	79	25
20– 59	62	90	87	82	105
60– 79	11	11	10	9	21
80–100	8	5	1	3	27

Now these categories will in many cases be overlapping ones (i.e., for example, an economist doing statistical analysis could well be engaged on economic forecasting), but it is still noticeable that specialisation does not appear to have spread very far. Thus in the categories of 60 per cent of working time and over there were only nineteen respondents doing operational work, sixteen on economic forecasting, eleven supplying economic information and twelve engaged on statistical analysis.

It is now time to consider just exactly what are all the specialist functions which business economists perform. These are summarised in Table 20.

TABLE 20. Specialist Functions Performed by Business Economists

	Weighting for all Respondents
Sales forecasting	11
Industrial market research	11
Economic analysis of competing companies	9
Environmental forecasting	9
Pricing problems of industry	7
Analyses of distribution problems	5
Capital projects	8
Advice on primary commodities	5
Security/investment analysis and forecasts	4
Analysis of supply problems	4
Production programmes	3
Analyses of services	2
Analysis of underdeveloped economies	3
Advice of foreign exchanges	3
Economic analysis of agriculture	2
Advice on trade and public relations	6
Others	8
	100

The table gives an indication of the variety of specialist functions which business economists perform, and it is weighted
according to the extent to which it is performed by respondents.
The table does *not*, however, show how the importance of
different functions varies to any *one* business economist. It is clear
from the table that there is a fairly wide range of functions
performed by business economists in Britain to-day. The major
importance of the marketing and selling functions compared to
others, e.g. production, is again illustrated, and it is worthwhile at this stage to summarise all the evidence for this. Putting
together all the illustrative data gives the following picture:

(1) Of the departmental attachment of business economists
not in Economics Departments 64 per cent was to the Marketing
function;

(2) of the other functional departments which co-operated
with Economics Departments the Marketing Departments were
most important with 40 per cent of Economics Departments
having close co-operation with them;

(3) A very significant proportion—38 per cent—of the work

of economists was initiated from the Marketing function; and

(4) Of the specialist functions performed by business economists 52 per cent were concerned with the Marketing function.

This situation can be sharply contrasted with the corresponding activities of business economists in the fields of capital investment analysis and analysis of production programmes where the position of business economists is shown in Table 21.

TABLE 21. Relationship of Business Economists to Capital Investment and Production Analysis

	Capital Investment	Production	Total
	(Per cent of respondents)		
(1) Departmental attachment of economists not in separate Economics Departments	12	2	14
(2) Close co-operation between Economics and other departments	12	6	18
(3) Initiation of work from other departments	11	10	21
(4) Specialist functions performed by individual economists	8	3	11

It is important to have some idea as to whether this pattern is likely to continue, with its implications for training. It is of course difficult to forecast likely future requirements which depend on many variables, but the topic is discussed in broad terms in Section VIII.

It is clear that one of the most important functions performed by business economists is forecasting, and it is interesting to examine this aspect of his work further. One important aspect is the length of the period ahead for which forecasts are made by economists. For respondents this is shown in Table 22.

It is clear from Table 22 that there is a fairly wide spread of periods for which forecasting is done. To obtain a probably more accurate answer to this question economists were asked to indicate the periods of forecasting performed in their organisations (i.e. not only by themselves). An indication of this is given in Table 23. Table 23 confirms that there are two broad types of forecasting being carried out in British industry to-day,

namely short-term and medium-term. This result is of some
significance for several reasons. Firstly, it gives some indication
of the type of forward planning being carried on in British industry (and by public bodies). Secondly, it has implications for the
training of economists. In particular, it is important to note that
different techniques are necessary for short-term forecasting
compared to medium and longer-term forecasting.

TABLE 22. Period Ahead for which Forecasts are made by
Individual Economists

	Majority of forecasts (Number of respondents)	Per cent	Some forecasts (Number of respondents)	Occasional forecasts (Number of respondents)
Under 6 months	28	11	24	8
6 months and under 1 year	48	21	47	13
1– 3 years	49	21	49	19
3– 5 years	25	10	32	18
5– 7 years	55	23	59	30
7–10 years	23	10	38	49
11–20 years	9	4	15	26
	237	100		

TABLE 23. Period Ahead for which
Companies Make Majority of Forecasts

	Per cent
Under six months	7
6–12 months	22
1– 3 years	26
3– 5 years	13
5– 7 years	26
7–10 years	3
11–20 years	3
	100

An attempt was made to discover the geographical fields of
interest of British business economists. The results for respondents are summarised in Table 24.

From this table it is seen that 22 per cent of respondents devote
60 per cent or more of their time to working on problems of

TABLE 24. Geographical Fields of Interest of Economists:
Britain and Overseas

Britain Overseas (% of working time)		Per cent of Respondents
0	100	4
20	80	8
40	60	60
80	20	50
100	0	28

countries overseas. This is fairly significant and it is worthwhile
detailing the type of overseas economies which are being studied.
This is done in Table 25.

TABLE 25. Overseas Economies Studied by
Business Economists

Region	Number of times mentioned	Per cent of total
Europe	79	31
North America	48	18
Asia/Australasia	46	18
Africa	38	15
Latin America	20	8
Middle East	19	7
Sino-Soviet	9	3

There is thus a fairly wide geographical spread of working
interests. It was thought worthwhile to relate these figures to
data of British exports. These are shown in Table 26. Though

TABLE 26. British Exports by Area of Destination
Monthly Averages (1965)

	£ million
North America	58
Western Europe	145
Latin America	13
Australia and New Zealand	33
Soviet Union and Eastern Europe	9
Total Sterling Area	137
Rest of World	31
Total	394

Source: Board of Trade

the figures are not precisely comparable it can be seen that there is a tendency for the two series to be directly related.

Perhaps the most important conclusion from the statistics, however, relates to the training of economists. The fact that there does exist a considerable demand for knowledge of economies outside Britain leads to the question of whether this demand is being catered for in British universities. There is now fairly widespread instruction on developing countries but, without being able to be dogmatic, it may be questioned whether adequate courses on European and North American economies are available to-day.

V. Effective Use of Economists

The question of the usefulness of economists in industry and (particularly) in government is one which has aroused considerable public interest in this country. The question of how effectively business economists themselves feel they are employed is an important one (though only, of course, one part of the broader controversy). The views of management were also sought and are dealt with in another report. Recipients of the questionnaire were asked whether their present employer fully utilised their know-how as economists and of the 262 who responded 137 (52 per cent) reckoned that their expertise was being fully utilised while 125 did not. This is a clear indication of dissatisfaction on the part of business economists. When effective use was related to type of organisation major differences were found. Thus 90 economists (54 per cent of respondents to this question) from the industrial section claimed that their abilities as economists were not being fully utilised while 18 economists (35 per cent of respondents to this question) in the commercial/financial sector said they were not being fully utilised; in the Government/public bodies sector the corresponding figure was 7 (35 per cent of respondents). This is fairly convincing evidence that economists in the industrial sector are by far the most ineffectively used. When effective use was related to size of organisation it was found that there was no noticeable correlation in any sector. The cause of ineffective use would thus appear to be a structural one rather than one of size. Particular reasons for ineffective use are considered below.

Recipients were also asked to indicate the impact of their work on the policy of their employers. Their answers are indicated in Table 27.

TABLE 27. Impact of Work of Economists on Policy

	Number of respondents	Per cent of total
Very substantial	47	18
Considerable	100	39
Moderate	87	33
Very slight	26	10

Care is needed in interpretating this table especially in relation to the immediately previous statement. Thus it could be, for example, that an economist whose expertise is being very fully utilised by his employer may still make only a moderate impact on policy. Clearly the impact which an economist can make on policy will depend on factors such as the structure of the industry in which his firm is operating (i.e. completely *independent* of the effectiveness with which his skills are being utilised). There are thus many influences at work behind the data of Table 27, and it is impossible to separate those which are 'internal' to the skill of the economist and those which are 'external'. It seemed possible that there might be significant differences in the impact of the economists's work according to the type and size of organisation for which he worked. On examination the type of employer made no great difference to the impact which the economist made; a greater proportion of economists in the commercial/financial field did, however, make 'very substantial' impacts than in the other two sectors. So far as size of organisation and impact of work are concerned no noticeable relationship was present. This is not a surprising finding as economists of different levels of seniority were being lumped together. It probably also reflects, however, the likelihood that other factors such as the structure of the particular industry influence the impact which *any* economist could make on policy.

A possibly more profitable line of inquiry is to consider directly the reasons for the ineffective use of economists. For respondents the answers are shown in Table 28.

TABLE 28. Reasons for Ineffective Use of Economists

	Number of times mentioned	Per cent of total
Reports not used	2	1
Reports not used properly	18	10
Ineffective reporting relationship	27	15
Function mis-directed	54	30
Ineffective co-operation with other departments	32	18
Others	47	26

The most important single reason is thus seen to be mis-direction of function. It must, of course, be remembered that this represents only the feelings of the economists, but insofar as it is a reflection of the true state of affairs the main blame must fall on the shoulders of management. It is easy to think of reasons why management in Britain to-day may not appreciate the best use to which economists can be put. It is a young profession and many managements may well have had little experience in the application of economics and economists to business problems. If this reason is correct then this source of ineffective use can be expected to diminish in the next few years. Management is of course ultimately responsible for the reporting relationships and inter-departmental co-operation of employees and therefore must share part of the blame for these sources of ineffective use. The immediate reasons, however, could well be different, such as the ignorance of colleagues in other departments of the contribution which economists could make, or the inability of the economist himself to explain himself to colleagues working in other functions.

When the various reasons for ineffective use were related to the different employing sectors it was discovered that the pattern did not vary in the sense that any single reason stood out as being especially important in any one sector. This suggests that the problems to be solved are much the same in all sectors, but in general they are more prevalent in the industrial sector.

On the question of inter-departmental co-operation it was thought worthwhile to consider the particular departments with which economists thought more-cooperation was desirable. For respondents the answers are given in Table 29.

TABLE 29. Improved Efficiency of Economists through
Closer Inter-departmental Co-operation

Closer co-operation between Economics Departments and	Much closer co-operation desirable No. of times mentioned	Per cent	Closer co-operation No. of times mentioned	Per cent
Board	21	13	27	10
Finance	25	16	43	16
Capital projects	25	16	41	15
Planning	25	16	37	14
Production	9	6	20	7
Supply	5	3	17	16
Marketing	17	11	43	16
Market Research	6	4	18	6
Distribution	6	4	15	5
Others	17	11	13	5

From this table it can be clearly seen that economists are anxious
to have close co-operation not only with functions to which
they are already closely attached (e.g. marketing), but *particularly* with functions to which their attachment was found to be
not especially strong. This is important for it suggests that
economists do feel that they can make stronger contributions to
the solution of problems of other functions in their organisations. The implication is probably that management have not
yet discovered the potential usefulness of the economist for these
other problems, though it is of course also possible that the
economist has too high an opinion about his own usefulness in
solving some business problems.

It was thought worthwhile to investigate the working
relationship of economists with one other specialist, namely the
accountants. For respondents the results are shown in Table
30.

TABLE 30. Working Relationships of Economists with Accountants

	Number
Closely co-ordinated	46
Useful liaison	96
Loose contact	64
No liaison	47
Others and no information	53

Table 30 shows that 44 per cent of respondents had no or only loose contact with the accountants in their firms. This is in line with the previous findings that a large proportion of economists thought that their co-operation with the Finance Department was inadequate. At least part of the blame for this state of affairs must rest with the management of the firms concerned.

The attitude of management is certainly a most important factor in the effective utilisation of the economist, and in an attempt to pin down the significance of contact with top management the proportion of economists' work initiated by the Board of Directors was related to the various reasons for the ineffective use of economists. The result is shown in Table 31. From Table 31 it can be seen that there is only a slight tendency for the expertise of economists to be more fully utilised the closer is their contact with the Board of Directors.

TABLE 31. Effective Use of Economists

Reasons for ineffective use of economists	Proportion of work initiated by Directors or Board—per cent						
	0–9	10–19	20–29	30–49	50–74	75–100	Total
Your reports are not used			1			1	2
Your reports are not used properly	5	4	5	1	1	2	18
Your reporting relationship does not ensure that your know-how is effectively utilised	8	4	6	2	3	3	26
Your actual *function* could be changed with advantage to the company's over-all efficiency	17	7	8	4	11	5	52
Co-operation with other departments is not as effective as it could be	9	6	5	2	5	2	29
Others	12	7	7	1	9	5	41
TOTAL	51	28	32	10	29	18	168

This analysis was taken further and the proportion of work initiated by the Board was related to the different types of

employer. It was found that there was a slightly higher proportion of work initiated by the Boards of industrial companies
compared to the other sectors. The size of the employing
organisation did not prove to be an important factor here, the
only noteworthy tendency being for the smaller industrial
companies (measured by turnover) to have a higher proportion
of work initiated by their Boards than larger industrial companies.

A further comparison was made between the proportion of
work initiated by the Board and the impact of the economist's
work on company policy. It was discovered that there was only
a slight tendency for work impact to vary directly with the
proportion of work initiated by the Board, suggesting again the
obvious conclusion that effective utilisation seems to depend on
several factors and not only on direct contact with the top policy
makers. Another finding which with the other findings tends to
the same conclusion, was that there was no apparent relationship between the proportion of work initiated by the economist
and his impact on company policy.

One factor in the effective utilisation of economists is an adequate supply of relevant books and other publications. The
adequacy of these for respondents is shown by broad type of
employer in Table 32.

TABLE 32. Provision of Books and Type of Employer

Attitude of Employer to provision of books etc.	Industrial	Commercial and Financial	Govern- mental and Public	No infor- mation	Total
Very liberal	65	30	9	18	122
Liberal	92	18	9	13	132
Cautious	18	6	4	3	31
Cheese-paring	2	2	1		5
No information	4	5		7	16
TOTAL	181	61	23	41	306

The table shows that more than one-tenth of employers adopt a
cautious or cheese-paring attitude to the supply of relevant
books. However, the impact of this on an individual economist's
effectiveness is very difficult to measure and, indeed, will vary

greatly according to circumstances, for requirements of books will vary greatly with the nature of the job being undertaken.

In order to discover more about what encouragement economists were being given they were asked to comment on their employer's attitude to the undertaking of research not immediately applicable to their job in hand. The replies are shown in Table 33, related to a broad classification of the economist's job.

TABLE 33. Attitude of Employers to Research not immediately applicable to their activities, and Nature of Job.

Nature of Job		Attitude of Employers				
Infor-mational	Analy-tical	Encouraging	Neutral	Discouraging	No information	Total
Per cent	Per cent					
0	100	12	11	1	1	25
20	80	70	56	10	10	146
60	40	33	37	10	4	84
80	20	7	14	2	3	26
100	0					
No information		4	4	2	15	25
TOTAL		126	122	25	33	306

The table does bring out one point fairly clearly. Employers tend to give greater encouragement to research to those economists who are engaged on predominantly analytical work. This is probably because such economists are doing work which is more clearly seen to be of value to the company than informational work (or possibly because the economists concerned are in a position more easily to persuade management to this effect!)

A most interesting question connected with the general question of utilisation is to consider how the economist's impact on company policy has changed in the last few years and to inquire how he expects it to change in the future. For respondents the answers are shown in Table 34.

It is clear from this table that the influence of economists has continued to increase markedly over the last ten years. Economists are also expecting that this should continue to be true over the next ten years, though this 'growth of influence' may not be so rapid as that experienced in the past decade.

TABLE 34.

Changing Importance of Economists in Company Policy. Last Ten Years

	2 years ago	5 years ago	10 years ago
Much more important role	30	69	97
More important role	161	97	47
Less important role	9	8	3

Changing Important of Economists in Company Policy. Next Ten Years

	2 years time	5 years time	10 years time
Much more important role	18	41	60
More important role	177	146	104
Less important role	6	2	1

An attempt was next made to relate the changing importance of the economist to the size and type of employing organisation. In the last few years respondents thought that economists had become more important in all sectors, the change being particularly marked from the situation of ten years ago in the industrial and commercial/financial sectors. No noticeable relationship was seen between changing importance and size of employing organisation.

The subject of future utilisation is discussed further in Section VIII dealing with career prospects.

VI. Qualifications and Training

In order that economists can be effectively utilised in business they must be properly trained. The profession being a young one it is important to discover whether they are receiving adequate training at university. Accordingly economists were asked several questions regarding the adequacy of their university training for the jobs which they were now carrying out. Firstly, however, economists were asked to rank the usefulness of several main areas of economics in their work. The results for respondents are summarised in Table 35.

C

TABLE 35. Usefulness of Selected Main Areas of
Economics to Business Economics

	Often Useful	Occasionally Useful	Never Useful
	(No. of times mentioned)		
Theory of firm—price and output	62	129	64
Theory of international trade	47	127	70
National income and social accounting	117	111	30
Money and banking	64	105	78
Public finance and fiscal policy	87	113	48
Business financing	91	119	46
Economics of developing countries	33	102	104
Theory of Customs Unions and free trade areas	34	114	87
Theory of firm—investment decision	76	117	62
Demand theory	89	126	41
Others	30	13	1

On the same lines information was sought on the usefulness
of individual concepts in economics. The answers are shown in
Table 36.

TABLE 36. Usefulness of Economic Concepts

	Frequent practical application	Useful concept	Useless concept
	(No. of times mentioned)		
Price elasticity of demand	87	176	9
Income elasticity of demand	84	171	13
Opportunity cost	96	135	29
Value added	77	146	32
The multiplier	36	177	43
Propensity to consume	60	148	45
Marginal revenue product	65	142	48
The speculative motive	36	123	90
Production function	38	133	70
Balanced growth	37	129	70
Liquidity preference	25	147	78
Trade creation and diversion	34	118	79
Others	28	87	116

The results are not unexpected. The importance of the marketing functions is again very apparent. Perhaps the most surprising feature about Table 35 is the large proportion of economists who find certain fields useless. This probably reflects the specialisation of job functions among business economists which has already reached such a stage that certain main fields of the subject are not covered in day-to-day work.

Economists were then asked to rank the teaching of main subjects which they had received in terms of its suitability for their present professional requirements. The results are shown in Table 37. The results are certainly illuminating for they show that, for a main user of economists, teaching in some whole fields is rather inadequate. (No argument is of course being put forward that teaching ought only to reflect usefulness in this sense.) In particular, Tables 35 and 37 show that National Income and Social Accounting and Business Finance which were found to be the two most useful fields were both rather inadequately taught.

TABLE 37. Adequacy of Teaching in Terms of Professional Requirements

	Fully adequate	Barely adequate	Not taught	Total
Theory of firm—price and output determination	134	95	4	233
Theory of international trade	158	58	3	219
National income	120	95	17	232
Money and banking	170	47	5	222
Fiscal policy	145	73	6	224
Business finance	57	110	63	230
Economics of developing countries	78	51	85	214
Theory of Customs Unions and free trade areas	99	51	66	216
Theory of firm—investment decision	64	127	38	229
Demand Theory	158	68	2	223
Others	16	17	9	42

A similar pattern emerges when certain main fields of statistics are considered. Economists were asked to indicate the usefulness of certain statistical techniques in their work, and to rank the adequacy of the teaching they received in these fields.

The results are shown in Tables 38 and 39. These two tables clearly indicate the inadequacy of the teaching of statistical methods to economists. (Again it should be clear that this is not a criticism of statisticians but of the syllabi which exist (or did exist) in British universities.)

Other evidence of the inadequacy of teaching is found when the specific techniques which economists have had to learn after leaving university are considered. These are summarised in Table 40.

TABLE 38. Usefulness of Statistical Techniques.

	Often useful	Occasionally useful	Never useful
	(No. of times mentioned)		
Analysis of trend and seasonal variation of time series	182	76	11
Analysis of variance	43	116	75
Simple linear regression	95	112	43
Multiple regression	42	93	93
Tests of hypothesis	28	73	110
Computational analysis	26	70	94
Other	35	19	3

TABLE 39. Adequacy of Teaching in Terms of Professional Requirements

	Fully adequate	Barely adequate	Not taught	Total
Analysis of trend and seasonal variation of time series	138	77	28	243
Analysis of variance	93	77	58	228
Simple linear regression	117	62	57	236
Multiple regression	49	83	92	224
Tests of hypotheses	54	69	91	214
Computational analysis	28	43	135	206
Other	13	16	12	41

Thus two-thirds of all respondents have had to spend time acquiring knowledge of economic forecasting and discounted cash flows. Yet both these techniques are perfectly respectable from an academic point of view and could easily be included in any economics degree course.

As a follow-up to these questions economists were asked what broad changes they would recommend in university courses. Their answers are shown in Table 41 related to the nature of the economist's job.

TABLE 40. Techniques which have had to be Acquired
Since Leaving the University

	Number of respondents
Economic forecasting	221
Discounted cash flow	202
Other methods of assessing capital projects	142
Security analysis	76
Statistical techniques	169
Various other techniques	87

TABLE 41. Changes in Training and Nature of Job.

Nature of Job		Changes recommended in university course				
Informational	Analytical	More theory	More Applied	No change	No view Expressed	Total
Per cent	Per cent					
0	100	2	16	5	2	25
20	80	4	97	30	15	146
60	40	4	53	13	14	84
80	20	1	12	4	9	26
100	0					
No view expressed		1	7	8	9	25
TOTAL		12	185	60	49	306

The data show that 72 per cent of respondents to this question wanted university courses to have more applied economics and less theory. However, this feeling does not seem to be influenced by the broad nature of the job which the economist is performing. At any rate there is no sign that economists whose job has a high analytical content are any more enthusiastic about theory.

It was thought interesting to investigate the business economist's reading habits especially among the learned journals, for this should give clues to the nature of his continuing training. The results are shown in Table 42.

A certain dissatisfaction with economic theory can be deduced from this table which shows the very low usage of the learned

TABLE 42. Use of Journals by Economists

	Consult:	
	Regularly	Occasionally
	Number of Respondents	
Board of Trade Journal	173	98
Bank reviews	150	114
Ministry of Labour Gazette	110	114
U.N. Publications	81	136
The Banker	67	100
Investment Analysist	45	59
Economic Journal	42	113
Journal of Industrial Economics	37	96
Journal of Royal Stat. Soc. Series A	34	112
Bankers' magazine	29	41
Economica	21	95
I.M.F. Staff Papers	20	55
Journal of Management Studies	19	57
Oxford Econ. Papers	18	97
Journal of Econ. Abstracts	18	38
American Economic Review	17	65
Manchester School	15	98
Review of Economics and Stats.	11	35
Econometrica	9	45
Review of Economic Studies	5	57
Quarterly Journal of Economics	5	35
Scottish Journal of Pol. Econ.	3	44
Journal of Pol. Econ.	2	33
Others (various)	155	18

journals amongst business economists. It is probable that the low usage reflects a poor assessment of the contribution which academic economists make to the practical problems confronting business economists. It may be, however, that the poor estimate applies rather more to the subject matter acceptable to the Editors of the learned journals rather than to the capabilities of academic economists, for they contribute substantially to the Bank Reviews which, as Table 42 shows, are fairly heavily read. However there would certainly seem to be cause for concern amongst business and academic economists when only 14 per cent of business economists regularly consult the U.K.'s leading learned journal—*The Economic Journal*—and only 51 per cent consult it at all. By an oversight on the part of the authors the National Institute of Economic and Social Research Journal *Economic Review* was omitted from the list suggested to respondents. Only a very few respondents added this journal in the spaces provided for journals read but not listed. Given the valuable contribution the journal makes to the analysis of current economic trends this is surprising and may be taken as a further indication of a tendency on the part of many business economists to 'stick to the primary sources'.

The same theme of lack of rapport between the two branches of the profession emerges when the attitude of business economists to conferences of business economists and university refresher courses as ways of equipping business economists to perform their duties more effectively are considered. While 235 respondents expressed support for conferences of business economists, only 179 thought the university refresher courses would be useful, and 107 thought that such courses would be of little or no use. The overwhelming reason adduced for this was that the techniques and concepts taught at university were unlikely to be relevant. There was, however, considerable support (200 respondents) for conferences which brought business and academic economists together, probably reflecting the belief that two-way communication was valuable for the development of the profession as a whole. That 35 respondents who favoured periodic conferences of business economists alone did not favour joint conferences with academics does, however, indicate the extent to which doubts exist about the value of academic contributions.

VII. Remuneration and Conditions of Service

Information on salaries is not always easy to obtain but economists taking part in this survey proved very willing to provide data, the response rate being very high. Salaries (applicable to U.K. mid-1965) are shown in Table 43 related to age.

From this table it can be seen that the modal salary range is £2000–£2500 p.a. and the median salary is £2386 p.a. The salaries of 58 per cent of respondents are in the range £1750–£3500 p.a. The table also indicates that there is quite a strong relationship between salary and age, notwithstanding the relative youth of the profession and the present shortage of economists. A possible explanation for this is that very competent young economists may have been promoted out of pure economics jobs into managerial posts, and can no longer be classified as economists. Business economists would still appear to be well paid in comparison to members of other professions, however, for Table 43 shows that by their later thirties about one-fifth of respondents were earning over £4500 p.a., one-half were earning over £3000 p.a. and three-quarters were earning over £2500 p.a.

TABLE 43. Age and Salary.

Salary £ per annum

Age	Below 1000	1000 and below 1250	1250 » 1500	1500 » 1750	1750 » 2000	2000 » 2500	2500 » 3000	3000 » 3500	3500 » 4000	4000 » 4500	4500 » 5000	Over 5000	No information	Total
20–22		1	3											4
23–25		11	9	3	1	1								25
26–28	1	1	9	9	8	4	1						1	34
29–31			2	6	13	17	7	2	1					48
32–35		1		2	11	21	18	12	6	4			2	77
36–40			1		3	6	13	7	4	3	5	4	2	48
41–45			1	1	3	5	1	6	2	4	3	5	2	33
46–50					1	3	3	3	1	2		5	1	19
51–59	1					1	5	1	3		1	1	1	13
60												1		1
No information			1			1	1		1					4
TOTAL	2	14	26	21	40	59	49	31	18	13	9	15	9	306

There is some evidence (from both firms and individual business economists) that the twelve months immediately following the conduct of this survey saw a substantial upward revision of the salaries of economists in industry, commerce and the public sector. These increases were at least partly in response to the rapidly expanding demand for economists in 1965 and 1966. Thus the salary position of economists related to that of other professions is probably rather more favourable than these 1965 figures suggest.

There is a fairly noticeable positive relationship between class of degree and salary among business economists. This is shown in Table 44 for respondents. From Table 44 it is seen that 76 per cent of respondents with first-class degrees earned over £2500 p.a., 46 per cent of those with upper-seconds earned over the same amount, as did 36 per cent with lower-seconds, 52 per cent with unclassified seconds, and 31 per cent with third-class degrees.

TABLE 44. Salary and Class of Degree.

Class of Degree	Below 1000	1000 and below 1250	1250 " 1500	1500 " 1750	1750 " 2000	2000 " 2500	2500 " 3000	3000 " 3500	3500 " 4000	4000 " 4500	4500 " 5000	Over 5000	No information	Total
First			2			3	6	6	3	2	2	3	2	29
Upper Second		4	12	7	15	18	13	10	4	7	5	6	2	103
Lower Second	1	7	7	8	11	13	11	7	3	1	1	3	1	74
Unclassified Second		1	2	2	3	4	4	3	1	2	1	1	1	25
Third		1	1	2	4	3	2	2	1					16
Other	1	1	1		2	1	2	2	1	1			1	13
TOTAL	2	14	25	19	35	42	38	30	13	13	9	13	7	260

Salary £ per annum

There is a certain puzzle regarding the achievement of respondents with unclassified seconds, but two possible explanations are (a) that Oxford and Scottish graduates (where second-class degrees have been unclassified) do relatively better; (b) that people who do well but have lower-seconds report their class as unclassified second as a result of doing well! Since age has been correlated with salary it was decided to eliminate this factor by relating salary and class of degree within an age group. The age group 32–35 years was chosen and the results are shown in Table 45.

TABLE 45. Salary and Class of Degree (Age Group 32–35 Years)

Class of degree obtained	Present Salary £ per annum													Total
	Below 1000	1000 and below 1250	1250"–1500	1500"–1750	1750"–2000	2000"–2500	2500"–3000	3000"–3500	3500"–4000	4000"–4500	4500"–5000	Over 5000	No information	
First					1	3	1	1		1			1	8
Upper Second			1	4	9	6	4	2					1	27
Lower Second	1		1	5	5	6	4	1						23
Unclassified Second					2	2	2	1		1				8
Third				1	2		1	1						5
Other				1						1				2
No information					2	1				1				4
TOTAL	1		2	11	21	18	12	6		4			2	77

The tendency for salary and class of degree to be positively correlated is now not so strong. It is very noticeable that respondents with unclassified seconds again do particularly well.

The relationship between salary and mobility is obviously a question requiring analysis and for respondents the 'gross' relationship is shown in Table 46. There is no obviously close relationship from the data of Table 46. On *prima facie* reasoning this is not exceptional for salary adjustments inside an industrial or commercial organisation are made much more easily than, say, at a university. Thus at a time of scarcity of business economists a firm, aware of the market situation, is likely to be quick to ensure that competent economists cannot be enticed away by the offer of higher salaries. Table 46, however, could show the lack of positive relationship for another reason, namely that it takes no account of the age of the economist which has been found to be an important factor determining salary. It is in fact likely that the lack of distinct relationship is due to a combination of these two factors.

TABLE 46. Salary and Mobility

No. of firms respondent has been employed with	Salary £ per annum													Total
	Below £1000	1000 and below 1250	1250 and below 1500	1500 and below 1750	1750 and below 2000	2000 and below 2500	2500 and below 3000	3000 and below 3500	3500 and below 4000	4000 and below 4500	4500 and below 5000	Over 5000	No information	
1	1	10	15	9	13	22	19	8	5	2		4	6	114
2		2	8	9	12	17	14	9	4	7	2	6	1	91
3				1	9	9	7	8	6	1	3	2	2	48
4				1	2	3	3	2	1	1				16
5						1	2	1		2		2		8
6						2	1							3
No information	1	2	3	1	2	6	4	2	1		3	1		26
TOTAL	2	14	26	21	40	59	49	31	18	13	9	15	9	306

The relationship between salary and type of employer is of much interest to-day because of the increasing employment of economists in all main sectors of the economy. The results are shown in Table 47.

The results are rather surprising. They show that there is a fairly pronounced tendency for salaries in Government/public sector employment to be higher than those in financial/commercial organisations while these in turn are higher than in industrial firms. Thus 65 per cent of Government/public body economists had salaries exceeding £2500 p.a., 59 per cent of financial/commercial economists had salaries above this level, and only 39 per cent of economists employed by industrial firms had salaries exceeding this. There are several possible explanations for this. One possibility is that the age distribution of economists is different in the three sectors. To eliminate the effect of this economists in one age group only were considered. The results are shown in Table 48.

TABLE 47. Type of Employer and Salary.

Type of Employer	Below 1000	1000 and below 1250	1250 ,, 1500	1500 ,, 1750	1750 ,, 2000	2000 ,, 2500	2500 ,, 3000	3000 ,, 3500	3500 ,, 4000	4000 ,, 4500	4500 ,, 5000	Over 5000	No information	Total
							Salary £ per annum							
Industrial	1	11	14	12	32	37	25	17	10	8	4	6	4	181
Financial & Commercial	1	3	6	3	4	6	14	6	5	3	4	4	2	61
Public and Governmental			1	1	1	5	4	6	2		1	2		23
No information			5	5	3	11	6	2	1	2		3	3	41
TOTAL	2	14	26	21	40	59	49	31	18	13	9	15	9	306

Table 48 shows that for this age group economists employed in the financial/commercial sector fare best and those in the industrial sector relatively worst. Care is needed in 'reading into' the statistics, however. A possible explanation of the relatively low industrial salaries is that in industrial firms the most competent economists may be promoted to managerial levels, and cease to be classified as economists at all. Nevertheless the main point is still valid for economists working as economists.

The relationship between salary and size of employer was also examined. So far as Government/public bodies are concerned there is no indication that size (measured by numbers employed) influence salary. Similarly there is scarcely any evidence that among financial/commercial employers salary was influenced by size (measured by numbers employed). Among industrial employers, when size was measured by employment no relationship was again evident. However, when size of industrial employers was measured by turnover a tendency for the larger firm to pay higher salaries was apparent. The results are shown in Table 49.

TABLE 48. Salary and Type of Employer (32–35 Age Group)

Type of Employer	Salary £ per annum													
	Below 1000	1000 and below 1250	1500 " 1250	1750 " 1500	2000 " 1750	2500 " 2000	3000 " 2500	3500 " 3000	4000 " 3500	4500 " 4000	5000 " 4500	Over 5000	No information	Total
Industrial	1		2	9	13	8	5	3	2					43
Financial & Commercial				1	2	4	3	3	2				1	16
Public and Governmental					3	2	3							8
No information				1	3	4	1						1	10
TOTAL	1		2	11	21	18	12	6	4				2	77

Table 49 shows that with firms having a turnover of less than £10 million only 25 per cent of economists earned over £2500 p.a., with firms having a turnover between £100 million and £300 million 44 per cent of economists earned over £2500 p.a. while, for firms having a turnover between £1000 million and £3000 million 45 per cent of economists earned over that figure. This is quite significant because it is very unlikely that the age factor could in this case produce any distortions to the relationship.

Salary can be related to job characteristics in different ways. Table 50 shows the relationship with the informational/analytical content of the job.

TABLE 49. Salary and Size (by Turnover) of Industrial Employer

Turnover (£m)	Salary £ per annum													
	Below 1000	1000 and below 1250	1250 " 1500	1500 " 1750	1750 " 2000	2000 " 2500	2500 " 3000	3000 " 3500	3500 " 4000	4000 " 4500	4500 " 5000	Over 5000	No information	Total
Under 10			2	2	8	5	2		1	1	2		3	26
11–30		1	2	2	4	8	3	3	1					24
31–60		4	2		2	5	3	3	3					22
61–100		1		1	5	2	3	1	1		1		1	16
101–300		3	1	2		8	3	3	1	3		3		27
301–500			1		4	2	3	1				1		12
501–750					2	1	1	1	1			1		7
751–1000														
1000–3000		1	4			5	2	2	1	1	1	1		18
3000 and over														
No information	1	1	2	5	7	1	5	3	1	3				29
TOTAL	1	11	14	12	32	37	25	17	10	8	4	6	4	181

Table 50 shows that there is no noticeable tendency for salaries to vary according to the analytical content of the job. This might be interpreted as suggesting that hard work can pay well. It is in fact possible that the ability to provide the correct information at the right time and in the right place is an important factor in business efficiency and is therefore rewarded just as highly as a more analytical type of job. On the other hand it is possible that the managements of some firms are not able to accurately assess the contribution which economic analysis can make to the solution of business problems. The explanation is probably a combination of the above possibilities.

When the geographical specialisations of economists are related to their salaries the results are as in Table 51.

TABLE 50. Salary and Job Characteristics

Job Characteristics Informational %	Analytical %	Below 1000	1000 and below 1250	1500 " 1250	1750 " 1500	2000 " 1750	2500 " 2000	3000 " 2500	3500 " 3000	4000 " 3500	4500 " 4000	5000 " 4500	Over 5000	No information	Total
0	100		1	2	1	4	2	7	2	1	2	1	2		25
20	80	1	7	9	9	20	29	19	31	13	6	3	7	2	146
60	40		4	9	10	11	20	11	7	3	2	3	2	2	84
80	20	1	1	6	1	3	7	5			2				26
100	0														
No information			1			2	1	7	1	1	1	2	4	5	25
TOTAL		2	14	26	21	40	59	49	31	18	13	9	15	9	306

TABLE 51. Salary and Geographical Specialisation

Geographical Specialisation British %	Overseas %	Below 1000	1000 and below 1250	1500 " 1250	1750 " 1500	2000 " 1750	2500 " 2000	3000 " 2500	3500 " 3000	4000 " 3500	4500 " 4000	5000 " 4500	Over 5000	No information	Total
0	100		1	2	1	2		3	1		1		2		13
20	80		2	3	1	3	3	4	3	3	2			1	25
40	60		1	2	3	2	4	10	3	1	2		1	1	30
80	20		4	9	10	18	36	20	16	10	4	7	9	2	145
100	0	1	5	9	6	14	14	6	6	4	2	1		1	69
No information		1	1	1		1	2	6	2		2	1	3	4	24
TOTAL		2	14	26	21	40	59	49	31	18	13	9	15	9	306

This table shows the interesting tendency for the salaries of economists who specialise in overseas economies to be rather higher than those for economists concerned mainly with the British economy. This could be due to a relative shortage of economists with expert knowledge of overseas economies, but it is also likely that it is due to the possibility that such economists will have worked overseas and their salaries tend to be rather higher as a consequence.

Most people obtain some sort of fringe benefits which vary greatly between occupations. Fringe benefits of business economists are shown in Tables 52 and 53.

TABLE 52. Fringe Benefits of Business Economists.

Additional fringe benefits as proportion of gross salary	
Per cent	No. of respondents
0–4	75
5–9	129
10–19	64
20–29	12
30–39	5
40–49	1
50 and above	—
No information	20

TABLE 53. Business Economists'
fringe Benefits Compared with those of others in
Company of same Seniority

Much greater	2
Greater	23
Same	186
Less	40
Much less	10
No information	17

The results are hardly surprising and need no elaboration. There is no significant relationship between fringe benefits as a proportion of salary and salary levels.

The hours of work of economists were considered and in Table 54 are shown related to salary levels.

TABLE 54. Salary and Hours Worked by Economists

Hours worked per day	Salary £ per annum													Total
	Below 1000	1000 and below 1250	1250 " 1500	1500 " 1750	1750 " 2000	2000 " 2500	2500 " 3000	3000 " 3500	3500 " 4000	4000 " 4500	4500 " 5000	Over 5000	No information	
5 hours						1	1							2
6 hours		1		1	3		1				1			7
7 hours	2	5	14	9	20	14	15	9	2		2	2		94
8 hours		7	8	6	13	34	19	10	7	3	2	7	2	118
9 hours		1	2	4	4	6	7	8	6	3	3	2	1	47
10 hours			1			3	4	2	2	6	1	1	1	21
Others			1			1	1	1	1	1		3		9
No information				1			1	1					5	8
TOTAL	2	14	26	21	40	59	49	31	18	13	9	15	9	306

There is a slight tendency for salary to increase with hours worked. No very strong causal connection could be easily asserted. It is quite likely that some economists attain senior positions with high salaries as a result of doing well and may in consequence have to work longer hours.

The relationship between the economist's salary and his impact on general company policy was next considered. The resulting relationship is shown in Table 55.

There is seen to be a tendency for salary to vary directly with impact on company policy. This to some extent shows an interesting tendency for the estimation of the economist's worth to the company as seen by management (through his salary) to coincide with the economist's own estimation of his value to the company. However, bearing in mind his already-noted indications of dissatisfaction in this respect this argument cannot be pressed. Finally in this analysis of salaries the expected relationship between salary and the proportion of work initiated by the economist himself is seen in Table 56.

D

TABLE 55. Salary and Impact on Company Policy.

Impact of work on company policy	Salary £ per annum													
	Below 1000	1000 and below 1250	1250–1500	1500–1750	1750–2000	2000–2500	2500–3000	3000–3500	3500–4000	4000–4500	4500–5000	Over 5000	No information	Total
Very substantial	1	3		2	3	4	6	9	4	3	4	8		47
Considerable		3	11	4	16	20	15	8	8	4	4	3	4	100
Moderate		2	9	12	12	24	14	8	1	1	1	2	1	87
Very slight	1	5	4	2	4	3	3	1	2	2				26
TOTAL	2	13	24	20	35	51	38	26	14	10	9	13	5	260

TABLE 56. Salary and Proportion of Work Initiated by Economist

Per cent of work initiated by self	Salary £ per annum													
	Below 1000	1000 and below 1250	1250–1500	1500–1750	1750–2000	2000–2500	2500–3000	3000–3500	3500–4000	4000–4500	4500–5000	Over 5000	No information	Total
0–9	1	7	16	7	2	15	10	1				2		61
10–19		4	5	5	15	11	10	6		2	1	2	1	62
20–29		1	4	2	9	10	7	2	3	4		3	2	47
30–49		1		2	8	10	2	13	4	2	3	1	1	47
50–74				4	2	4	5	3	4			2		24
75–100						3	6	3	4	2	4	3		25
No information	1	1	1	1	4	6	9	3	3	3	1	2	5	40
TOTAL	2	14	26	21	40	59	49	31	18	13	9	15	9	306

VIII. Career Prospects

A useful way to start analysing the career prospects of business economists is to consider the growth in demand over the past few years and the likely changes in demand for the coming few years. Economists were asked to give details of how the employment of economists in their own organisations had changed over the past ten years. For respondents the results are shown in Table 57.

TABLE 57. Change in Recent Employment of Economists.

Actual Increase	Last 2 years	Last 5 years	Last 10 years
Nil	78	46	24
1–4	120	92	65
5–9	20	25	26
10–14	8	14	15
15–19	1	3	3
20–24	1	3	3
25–29		3	1
30–34			2
35–39		1	1
40 and over	2	1	4

The data show that in the last ten years the expansion of employment of economists in the respondents' organisations has been over 900, of which 650 has taken place in the last two years (there will be some double-counting due to more than one respondent being employed by the same firm). The big acceleration in the growth of demand has thus taken place only in the last year or two. It is instructive to discover the reasons for the increase. Economists themselves have indicated their own reasons for this which are shown in Table 58.

The main reasons are seen to be changes in the attitudes of management and the growth in complexity of the employing organisation. It may well be that this growth in complexity is due more to a broadening of the firm's interests—e.g. by new products and technological changes—rather than from a mere growth in size for this latter influence is, by itself, seen by economists as being a relatively unimportant one.

Another indication of the growth in demand for economists

TABLE 58. Reasons for Recent Changes in Employment of Economists

	First Choice	Second Choice	Third Choice	Fourth Choice	Expected Change: One Choice Only
(a) The industry of which your company is a member has grown in complexity and the economist can make a valuable contribution to the understanding of the basic working of the industry	6	15	6	3	52
(b) Your firm in particular has grown in complexity and the economist can make a valuable contribution to the solution of some of the problems it faces	37	13	13	7	98
(c) There has been a change in the attitude of top management who are now realising that economists can make contributions to the solution of business problems	53	18	7	5	107
(d) The structure of industry and the economy in general has become more complex and the economist is useful in interpreting/analysing this general industrial environment and its possible effect on any one company	16	20	12	9	78
(e) An extension of the division of labour as your company has grown in size	12	14	3	7	67
(f) The requirements and opportunities which arise from the increasing influence of government and government agencies in economic and industrial affairs	10	6	10	7	61
(g) Others	34	1		1	52

in the last five years can be obtained by considering advertisements in the press. Accordingly, advertisements in *The Economist* for economists to be employed in industry, commerce and the public service were analysed, with an attempt being made to eliminate re-advertisements. The results are shown in graphical form in an Appendix along with comparative data showing the growth in advertisements for academic economists. The rate of growth exhibited by these advertisements is greater than that experienced by respondents; 248 posts were advertised in 1964 and 366 in 1965. This rate of growth is, however, clearly much faster than that shown over the whole past decade. Returning to the data provided by respondents it seems in fact that the annual rate of growth in demand over this period has been around $3\frac{1}{2}$–4 per cent.

Since the current state of the market for economists has aroused much interest it was thought useful, as part of the investigation, to approach these firms and other institutions (non-academic) which have recently been in the market for economists. One way of carrying out such an investigation is to approach firms and institutions who have recently advertised for economists. Accordingly a short questionnaire was sent to all firms and institutions who advertised in *The Economist* between 1 January 1965 and the end of June 1965 with some attempt being made to eliminate repetitions of advertisements for the same post (such attempts are unlikely to have been wholly successful).

In general terms the questionnaire was designed with a view to obtaining some guide to:

(a) the growth of the market;
(b) reasons for such growth;
(c) where the new economist would fit into the organisational structure of the company;
(d) the types of experience and qualifications which were considered advantageous for the advertised post(s);
(e) to what extent economists were involved in the actual appointment(s);
(f) some impressions which the firm had regarding the suitability of applicants for the advertised post(s);
(g) the number of applicants, number interviewed, and whether an appointment was made;
(h) source of appointed person.

General Nature of Post

Questionnaires were sent out regarding 119 advertised posts. The rate of response was 53 per cent. For over 62 per cent of the advertised posts the appointment was for a new post. This clearly illustrates the growth in the total demand for business economists. The 'fact' that 38 per cent of the advertised posts were for replacement purposes also does not take full account of the possibility that some of these vacancies have arisen because of the increased demand from other firms leading to some economists leaving their existing firms. (Over the six month period it is of course also true that some of this aspect will have been accounted for by the presence of an advertisement for a replacement for an economist who has replied to an earlier advertisement of another firm and has been hired by that firm.) This aspect of the problem will be expanded later when the question of the source of the appointed economist is considered.

Reasons for Creation of New Post

Concerning the question of the reasons for the growth of the market the questionnaire asked firms to give, in their own words, the reasons for the creation of the new posts. From the replies 55 per cent of the firms wishing to create new posts stated that their reason was the general expansion of the firm's activities. Another 40 per cent of these firms stated that their reason was the increased requirements of various departments for the service of economists. There is obviously some overlapping in these two broad explanations (and we attempted to take account of it), but the distinction is useful. The increased demands for the services of economists from some departments *can* of course come from the fact that departments (and so the company) has increased in *size*, but also from the possibility that users of economists have become more aware of the contribution that economists can make to the solution of their problems. (It was not possible to achieve a useful breakdown of the individual departments requiring additional services of economists from the replies received.) Also it is of course possible that behind these two main reasons there lie other (though related) explanations not specifically brought out in the replies. For example, it could be that the increased requirements from certain departments could stem not from a better appreciation of the value of economists in solving their business problems but from, say, the increased requirements of information from Government departments concerning, perhaps, future production or investment. Similarly it could be a change in the attitude of top management which has led to a certain department using the services of economists to a greater extent.

Organisational Position of Advertised Post

An attempt was made in the questionnaire to discover—very broadly—how the advertised post would fit into the organisational structure of the company. From the total number of replies 17 per cent stated that the post was for a new department (in all cases where there was a new department *and* a new post the appointed economist would work in the new department). In 34 per cent of the cases the appointment was to an existing Economics Department and in 28 per cent of cases the appointment was to some other department. There is thus discernible a fairly noteworthy tendency to keep economists together in specialist departments of their own rather than disperse them throughout the various functional departments which they may be serving. From the limited evidence it also appears that firms are continuing to do this as they expand the number of economists employed and when they take on economists for the very first time.

Role of Economist in Appointment

The replies to the questions concerning the role of the economist in the appointment showed that in 60 per cent of cases an economist was involved in the decision to advertise the post and in 59 per cent of the cases an economist was concerned in the actual selection of the successful candidate. Care is needed in interpreting these figures. In particular, in assessing the importance of the economist in the processes we do not know from the replies whether an economist was the *instigator* of the idea to advertise the post or whether he was merely consulted, nor whether he had a major influence on the choice of the successful candidate. Regarding what is probably the most interesting aspect of this question, namely the decision to advertise for a new post, the evidence does not show that the involvement of the economist was significantly different from that regarding the decision to advertise an existing post.

Qualifications and Experience for Advertised Post

Regarding qualifications all firms asked for a degree in Economics or related subject. In addition 50 per cent of the firms who replied requested some qualification or expertise in statistics or econometrics. Very few firms specified the length of experience as a working economist which was considered desirable, but 30 per cent of firms did request some experience. So far as broad fields of experience are concerned the vast majority of the firms which did specify this requested industrial experience. (This was to be expected as the majority of the total replies came from industrial/manufacturing firms and nationalised industries.) It does, however, mean that the demand for economists with particular experience in financial institutions and in consulting work was relatively low in the period. As regards experience by specialist functions (e.g. expertise in economic forecasting) the advertisements themselves and the replies to the questionnaires clearly show that such experience is of secondary importance, for it was very seldom specified. Regarding salary a range of figures was mentioned in the advertisements of 46 per cent of the firms. Of these firms the salary or salary range offered by 40 per cent of this number was either in the range £2000–£2999 or in some other range which approached £3000.

An interesting question is the qualifications and experience desired for the new posts, for this could throw light on the techniques likely to be in highest demand in the future. The replies show that there was some difference in the requirements of qualifications in statistics or econometrics. Of those firms advertising new posts over 52 per cent required a qualification in statistics while the proportion of replacement jobs requiring statistics was nearly 44 per cent.

Suitability of Applicants

Firms were asked to give their impressions about the suitability of applicants, particularly with regard to their qualifications and experience. Fifty-eight per cent of firms claimed that most of their applicants were inadequate on at least some aspect(s), and a further 9 per cent of the firms found all their applicants inadequate on some aspect(s). The firms specifying in more detail the nature of the inadequacies pointed out that most of these come from (a) inadequate degree—both subject and grade, and (b) lack of experience in the relevant broad field. From the comments of the firms it would be fair to say that they receive many applications which do not begin to satisfy the requirements in the advertisement—for example applications were received from people without a degree in Economics or any related subject, and/or with no experience at all in the required field.

Applications Received

Regarding applications received for the advertised posts 19 per cent of the firms received twenty or more applications for the advertised post, 14 per cent received between fifteen and nineteen applications, 22 per cent received between ten and fourteen applications, 23 per cent received between five and nine applications, and 14 per cent received between one and four applications. In veiw of the special interest in those posts for which some experience in statistics/econometrics was considered necessary it was thought useful to relate such posts with the corresponding number of applications to the numbers of applicants for the posts not requiring expertise in statistics. However, no discernible relationship was found between the requirement or non-requirement of statistics and the number of applications. Clearly other factors also had a big influence on the decision-making process of applying for the advertised posts, and these were sufficiently strong to overcome the probable effect of a relatively greater shortage of economists with statistical expertise. There are obviously many factors influencing a person's decision to apply for any particular post, e.g. salary offered, prospective promotion, location of job. In order to probe more deeply into this question the firms which received twenty and more applications were examined, and related to the others. This showed that there were no noticeable differences in the salaries offered by this group compared to the rest; also this group did not advertise salaries to a significantly greater extent than the total. Further, the distribution between public and private sector posts was comparable to that of the total, with public sector relatively slightly predominant in the group. On examination of the individual companies in this group it was fairly clear that, in relation to the total, they were organisations either with a well-established Economics Department or were organisations where the economist, *prima facie*, seemed capable of playing an important role. In relation to the total the organisations in the group also would appear to have a higher future growth potential.

Applicants Interviewed

It might seem that further indications of the adequacy of applicants may be obtained by looking at the numbers actually interviewed. Eight per cent of firms interviewed between ten and fourteen applicants, 7 per cent of firms interviewed between five and nine applicants, and 42 per cent of firms interviewed between one and four applicants. Overall 828 known applications were received and 300 were interviewed. Thus to take the case already looked at in the previous section—the group of firms with twenty applicants and over—the organisations in this group did *not* tend to interview a relatively high number of candidates. (This is of course logically quite consistent; out of a large number of applicants there may be one or two outstandingly well-qualified people. Thus the need to interview many of the others is eliminated. Similarly a firm which receives rather less applicants may well not have any outstanding candidates and so have to interview several of roughly the same qualifications because of the extra difficulty in deciding between them.) Further, there does not appear to be any significant relationship between the views of management of the firms regarding the general suitability of candidates and the numbers asked for interview. This could well be explained by the

hypothesis put forward above. The lack of any simple explanation of the numbers interviewed probably reflects the many
variables on both the supply (applications) and demand
(management) sides leading up to this eventual figure. Management will differ in their methods of judging candidates and,
probably more important, economists seem to have very strong
views about the relative attractiveness of different organisations.
This is reflected very clearly by the fact that the organisation
which received the largest number of applicants obtained over
eighty, as opposed to nil from the organisation with the smallest.

Appointment

A further indication of the state of the market may be obtained
from the data on whether an appointment was actually made.
Sixty per cent of the firms actually made an appointment, over
34 per cent did not make an appointment, and the rest had not
yet come to a decision.

The obvious deductions from these figures are (1) that there is
a marked shortage of suitably qualified economists and (2) that
although this is the case management is determined not to make
appointments at all costs when only unsuitable candidates
present themselves. Regarding the relationship between the
types of qualifications and experience desired and the decision
to make an appointment, there is no clear relationship between
the cases where no appointment was made and the requirement
of any particular qualification. It might have been expected, for
example, that a shortage of economists with statistical qualifications would have been reflected in a relatively large number of
cases where no appointment was made being where a statistical
qualification was required. The absence of such a relationship
probably reflects some factors discussed already such as the
greatly varying popularity of organisations with applicants. One
interesting relationship did emerge from the statistics. This was
a tendency for the cases where no appointment was made to be
replacement posts rather than new posts. This suggests two
factors at work (1) the general shortage of adequately-qualified
economists, so that firms are having difficulty in obtaining
replacements of the same calibre and (2) that where a new post

is being created the standard required by the organisation before it will make an appointment may be more flexible (in a downward direction!)

Source of Appointed Economist

The question of the source of the appointed economist is of considerable interest in assessing the market situation. Of the firms which made an appointment, in 74 per cent of cases the appointed person came from a similar post in another firm, and in the rest of the cases the appointment was from other sources (usually left unspecified). These statistics do reflect the great pressure on the market at the moment, especially when taken in the context of the fact that over 61 per cent of the posts were *new* ones. *In fact, the total number of appointments made (38) was less than the total number of new posts becoming available (40).* The figure of 74 per cent is also relatively very high because only 36 per cent of firms specifically requested working experience.

There was no noticeable tendency for those people taking up appointments from similar posts in other firms to prefer new or replacement posts.

Future Demand

It is now opportune to examine the expected change in demand for economists. The changes expected by economists themselves are shown in Table 59. The data indicate that economists expect a net increase in demand of over 500 in the next two years and a net increase of around 950 in the next ten years in their own firms. As before some double-counting is exhibited in these figures. On the other hand there is another factor which suggests that the prospective increase may be higher; this is because no account has been taken of firms which do not employ economists at present deciding to employ them in future. It is reasonable to expect that more managements will come round to the view that economists can contribute to the solution of their problems if past changes in their attitudes are considered. Thus the extended rate of growth foreseen by economists, which is again $3\frac{1}{2}$–4 per cent over the next decade, is likely to be on the low side. It may be supposed that, on present evidence, the prospects over the next couple of years can be seen fairly clearly, but that over a whole decade prospects are much more difficult to project. It is noteworthy that the rate of growth foreseen by economists in the next two years is much higher than that foreseen for the whole decade. It is difficult, however, to see how the growth rate can fall off so sharply in these later years. *Prima facie* it seems unlikely that a near-saturation point in the employment of economists will have been reached by then.

TABLE 59. Expected Change—Future Employment of Economists

Possible Decrease	Next 2 years	Next 5 years	Next 10 years
1–4	8	3	3
5–9	1	2	
Over 10			1
No Change	67	20	13
Possible Increase			
1–4	123	110	68
5–9	19	37	38
10–14	5	11	17
15–19	1	3	8
20–24	1	1	2
25–29		1	3
Over 30			2

Regarding the reasons for the expected growth economists again state that the most important ones are the changing attitudes of management and the growth in complexity of the firm. The increasingly complex nature of the general industrial environment is expected to become a relatively more important reason than it is to-day.

Economists and General Management

Another vitally important aspect of the business economist's career pattern is his prospects of entering general management. Of 258 respondents 211 (82 per cent) thought that they had prospects of entering general management. The rest were of the opinion that their prospects with their present employers were solely as economists. In fact the employers of only 42 respondents (17 per cent) adopted a policy which restricted the business economist to purely economics work. Another 86 (34 per cent) ensured that the economist had as good a chance as anyone else in a different function of entering general mangement. Finally the employers of 122 respondents (48 per cent) had a policy of letting potential managers 'emerge' without considering whether a person in any particular function had any particular advantages/disadvantages. Regarding the prospects of entering general management 67 respondents (26 per cent) thought that their chances of entering general management were higher than those of other specialists, 64 (24 per cent) thought their chances were lower, while 130 (50 per cent) thought their chances were the same as other specialists. A variety of reasons was put forward for this, the most important being the technical nature of the industry and the presence of a correct assessment by top management of the contribution which economists could make to general management. It is interesting to note, however, that economists now think that their chances of entering management are higher than they were in the past few years. This is illustrated in Table 60. When estimates of entering general management were related to size and type of employer it was found rather surprisingly that, in the opinion of respondents, neither factor affected the economist's chances. On examination it was found that 85 respondents (28 per cent of total sample) expressed a desire to enter general management.

TABLE 60. Present Chances of
Business Economists entering General Management Compared
to Recent Years

Chances	Compared to		
	2 years ago	5 years ago	10 years ago
Much higher	3	1	3
Higher	26	17	12
Same	142	84	40
Lower	45	58	27
Much lower	15	25	45
TOTAL	231	185	127

Economists were asked finally whether they were willing to move out of business economics altogether, and 173 (79 per cent of respondents to the question) asserted that they were prepared to do so. When asked whether they were prepared to move between firms as business economists 206 economists (91 per cent of respondents to the question) intimated their willingness to do so. The willingness of economists to move out of business economics was then related to type and size of employing organisation. Of those who replied to the question 122 (84 per cent) who were employed by industrial firms said they were prepared to move, 24 (65 per cent) of those employed by commercial/financial establishments were similarly inclined as were 9 (69 per cent) of those in Government/public service. The greater willingness of employees of industrial firms to move is thus apparent. Willingness to move from present employer was then related to salary, but no significant relationship was apparent. Similarly there was no significant relationship between the willingness to move of respondents and the degree of which they thought their ability was being utilised by their present employer. Finally, there was a slight tendency for the proportion of work of the economist which was initiated by the Board of Directors to be inversely related to their willingness to move from their present firm.

IX. Conclusions

This study has shown that there is no doubt that the economist has become an increasingly important figure in the British business scene in the last few years, both quantitatively and qualitatively. This has brought both opportunities and problems. This study has probably highlighted the problems but, it is hoped, in a constructive way. It has been discovered that the economist does not feel that he is being fully utilised by his employer. This is understandable with a new profession the value of which many managements as yet may know little. The answer clearly lies both in the growth of management education, and in a growth of the ability of the business economist to explain himself to a 'lay' manager. This is a two-way process but it seems clear that both parties will have much to gain by a better understanding of the problems of the other. The economist could then be fitted into the hierarchy of the firm in the most effective way. His function could be better adjusted to the requirements of the individual company (clearly these will vary greatly between firms and particularly between industries). With a better understanding with management his relationships with other specialists in his company could be made more efficient and his reports could be used to the best effect.

Regarding his actual functions there seems to be scope for further specialisation. The tendency to use economists predominantly in relation to the marketing function has been noted. There appears to be scope for his profitable utilisation in connection with other functions, e.g. finance and production. It can be anticipated that this will in fact occur in the next few years as his potential usefulness becomes more widely known. It is the possibility of a considerable expansion in his usage in these directions which leads to the conclusion that the forecasts of future demand by economists may be rather pessimistic.

Regarding training it is again the problems of the business economist which have been highlighted in the report. The growth of the profession has led to the need for techniques which are either not taught or not adequately taught at university and several of these, though perfectly respectable from an academic viewpoint, have had to be acquired after graduation. This does not, of course, lead to speedy utilisation of the economists' general ability in business, nor does it help to make management see his usefulness any more clearly. It is to be hoped that Economics Departments at the universities will quickly become aware of the importance of teaching such techniques as economic forecasting and discounted cash flows so that the economist can take his place in business more quickly and effectively.

The career pattern of a business economist seems to be similar to that of other specialists such as accountants. This pattern is likely to continue in the years to come. Many economists who expressed a willingness to leave the field of business economics gave a desire to enter general mangement as their aim. This is understandable, and may be expected to bring beneficial results for the efficient running of the organisation. There is in fact much to be said for regarding an Economics Department as a point from which the 'economic approach' is distributed throughout the company. The possibility of some economists moving into general management is likely to encourage this. Such movements are also likely to mean that the work of an Economics Department will be more closely integrated both with that of management and with that of other specialist functions. It seems, therefore, that business economists should regard with favour the elevation of some of their number to the ranks of management.

Certain problems of career structure still remain, however, and are likely to remain. Certain firms do not regard economists as management potential. This attitude may well be a correct one in certain industries where, for example, because of the technical nature of the industry, an economist is rather unlikely to become a successful general manager. There is another and perhaps more important point, however, which the present 'boom' has obscured. If all business economists regarded business economics simply as a convenient stepping-stone to general management, the development and standing of the profession might be impaired. (Comparisons can again be made with the accountancy profession where the continued presence of 'pure' accountants has certainly fostered the development of the profession—e.g. by developing new and refined tools of analysis.) It seems, therefore, that some sort of career structure within the field of business economics is necessary if the profession is to continue to develop most effectively. The profession might be in danger of losing its most able practitioners at the height of their powers. One recent development in this country might do something (at least) to slow down this tendency. This is the growth of the economic consultancy branch of the profession. This is at present indeed a very small branch. (Their advertisements were too small in number to be analysed separately in the Appendix.) However, it is a fast growing branch and, further, it can be maintained that the development of the profession will not depend on numbers alone but also on the skills of a few outstanding practitioners.

It may, at any rate, be concluded that the present difficulties should properly be regarded as teething troubles coming at the beginning of exciting developments.

E

APPENDIX

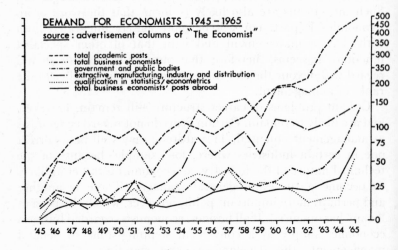

DEMAND FOR ECONOMISTS 1945 – 1965
source : advertisement columns of "The Economist"

---- total academic posts
····· total business economists
─·─· government and public bodies
─··─ extractive, manufacturing, industry and distribution
········· qualification in statistics/econometrics
──── total business economists' posts abroad

2

The Attitudes of Firms to the Employment of Economists

by K. J. W. Alexander

The Survey indicates the wide range of employment opportunity now open to economists and tells us something about the attitudes of economists to the firms which employ them. What about the attitude of firms to the employment of economists?

To get a general picture a postal questionnaire was sent to one hundred firms selected from *The Times* list of 300 top companies. In addition detailed discussions were had with eight employing firms. The covering letter which went with the questionnaire stressed that it should be completed by an appropriate member of top management who 'uses' economists and not by an economist. Similarly in visiting firms it was the 'users' not the economists with whom discussions were held. Fifty-six of the hundred firms replied, but of these thirteen did not complete the questionnaire, so that the analysis which follows is based upon information supplied by forty-three firms. Of these sixteen employed economists and twenty-seven did not. Of these twenty-seven, eight had previously employed an economist or economists, but no longer did so. A fairly high proportion of firms not employing economists indicated (in one or more ways) a very firm attitude in opposition to employing economists at present or in the future. The reasons for this will be examined in some detail.

A majority of 'employing' firms had less than ten economists on their staff. The distribution was as follows:

TABLE 1. Numbers Employed.

No. of economists on staff	1–4	5–9	10–14	15–19
No. of firms	7	4	3	2

Rather surprisingly eleven of these sixteen firms had distinct economic departments. There was a pronounced relationship between the size of firms measured by turnover and the number of economists employed; five of the nine firms employing four or fewer economists had an annual turnover of £60m or less. All of the firms with turnover of more than £100m organised their economists in a separate department, but so did six of the ten firms with turnover of £100m or less. As one would expect relationships between size measured by total employment and the number of economists employed are very much less pronounced.

Firms employing one or a few economists were more firmly convinced that the numbers employed would expand than were the firms employing ten or more.

The functional employment of economists reported by firms very closely paralleled that reported by economists themselves. The slightly higher weighting for the marketing function is presumably due to the predominance of industry in the sample of firms.

TABLE 2. Specialist Functions

Function	Estimate of percentage importance of function by	
	Economists	Firm
Marketing function	52	55
Production	26	24
Overseas, agriculture, etc.	22	21

There is encouragement for economists in both the range and the changing characteristics of the specialist function which firms have economists perform for them. The growth of corporate planning is a marked feature, as is the increasing need to have advice on relations between large corporations and governments. Many firms find that economists can perform an interpretative role in this increasingly important relationship. Particularly encouraging is the fairly widely held view that the training which economists receive equips them especially well for objective decision-taking.

In their estimates of the use of economists in the future we have already noted that amongst firms already employing economists it was those currently employing a few economists who were most convinced of future expansion. This may be taken as indicating that the decision to employ a few economists had proved fully justified. The same broad conclusions may be drawn from the fact that amongst employing firms a substantial majority saw an expanding need to employ economists whereas amongst firms not employing a substantial majority saw no such expansion taking place. Taking all firms together there was a small majority foreseeing no expansion of economists in their own firms. This small majority does not affect the overall estimate of expansion, however, as a substantial proportion of the firms making it up are 'non-employers', and no firms predicted a cut-back in their employment of economists.

There was evidence of considerable use of outside consultants to provide advice on economic matters. Six of the thirteen firms employing their own economists had also drawn on such outside help. The reasons given in such cases were either that the information required was highly specialised and therefore required knowledge not in the possession of the firms' own economists (e.g. market conditions in U.S.A.; particular industrial contacts required, etc.), or that the existing pressure on the firm's own economists justified additional expenditure on consultants to get quick results in particular cases. Of the twenty-seven firms not employing economists eight had employed consultants to advise on economic matters. The main reason for preferring consultants to economists permanently on the pay-roll was the obvious one that the jobs which required to be done were usually of short duration. This was sometimes related to the higher degree of specialism which could be called in from outside, and to the fact that consultancy provides firms with the help of a specialist *organisation* rather than the help of one economist.

The view that what economists have to offer a firm is only required intermittently seems to be the main explanation of why so many large firms do not employ their own economists. This view almost certainly reflects an underestimation of what economists do or could do. In the first instance many firms appear to think of the economist's potential contribution as solely on the marketing side. Indeed there is evidence that in many of those firms in which economists are now employed on production problems (e.g. capital projects) this has resulted from a 'contamination process' which started with economists being employed on marketing problems in the first instance. In the cases where there is an interest in the economic aspects of production problems reference is frequently made to the ability of the company secretary or of accountants to provide the guidance necessary. Some of the reasons given for not employing economists reflect the fairly common belief that all economists could produce would be statistics of the kind already readily available from government publications, the C.B.I., etc. Some firms go so far as to argue that it is their specialist nature which makes it unnecessary or impracticable for them to employ economists. Economic analysis geared to the understanding of a particular firm's problem seems to be an alien concept to some top managers. In only two of the firms responding was the presence of people with training in economics amongst the top management referred to, This may have been more common, however, as the information was volunteered, not specifically asked for.

Information about the training firms would wish their economics recruits to have had was collected from managers in the eight firms visited. Attitudes seemed rather mixed, even within companies. On the one hand there seemed fairly general support for the view that young economists knew far too little about business practice. In particular there was regret that they lacked knowledge of accounting practice and of the forms in which accountancy data is presented and analysed. Despite this a very strong preference was expressed for the graduate trained in 'pure economics' as distinct from the graduate whose training had been specifically geared to business or commerce. In some cases this preference seemed to be based on the view that such 'pure' training attracted the better intellects, leaving the thought that if this were not so, or if it could be changed, these firms would prefer graduates with a business training. Other firms preferred the 'pure' training on the grounds that it produced a superior and more multi-purpose graduate, with better powers of reasoning and analysis. One firm holding this view regarded a training in pure mathematics as almost as good as one in economics.

For project planning and investment decision the use of mixed groups of technologists, accountants and economists was a feature of a few of the largest firms. Ideally the economist members of such a team should have university training in both Economics and a science subject, although an A-level in a science-type subject has often to be accepted as fulfilling the technological requirement. A few firms encourage economist employees to take further training in statistics or, occasionally, in a technological subject. Training within the firm is rarely formal, though here may be a scheme by which the trainee moves around between departments. Most training is 'on the job', and there are many complaints about recent graduates' lack of expertise in the techniques of applied economics. The strongest form this took was the opinion that non-economist Arts graduates were just as good potential for economics work in business as the university trained economist. There was a fairly strongly expressed view that university training failed to show how much of the theory taught could be put to use. The concentration in the last year of training on what was called in one instance 'the higher theory' was criticised and the suggestion made that the emphasis at that stage ought to be on applied work. Although some of the views expressed here reflected a misapprehension as to the relationship between theoretical and applied work in economics, the criticisms bear serious consideration by academic economists concerned with the planning of degree courses.

Reference was also made by several 'users' to the discontent and dissatisfaction often expressed by young graduates in their early years in business employment. Although this discontent usually crystallised around complaints of a failure by the firm to use the young economist's talents fully, it was suggested that part of the trouble was that the graduate economist came from the university with a 'box of glittering tools which neither he nor anyone else knew how to use'. The unwillingness of one firm to employ graduates with First Class honours in economics seemed to be based on the view that this problem would be especially acute in their case. Here again there is a mixture of misunderstanding on the part of firms and weaknesses which the universities ought to pay attention to.

A great majority of firms considered that economics graduates were very good general management potential. In some cases the desirability of moving over from work as an economist to general management reflected doubts about the satisfaction and seniority which could be achieved through the exclusive performance of an economist's function. 'A good man will not be content to sit in the back room beyond the age of forty' was one way in which this view was expounded. Even in some of the larger firms employing economists there is no career structure for the majority of economists if they wish to remain with the firm and continue as economists. This reflects both the limited use which is made of economics in some firms and the embryonic state of the profession of business economist. A few firms have evolved a satisfactory career structure, however, and both extensions of the use of economics within firms and the competition for economists in scarce supply will shortly extend this development to other firms.

3

Economic Forecasting in the Esso Petroleum Company Limited

by Colin Robinson

The Company and How It Employs Economists

Esso Petroleum Company Limited is a subsidiary of Standard Oil Company (New Jersey) and is engaged in the marine transportation of oil products and refining and marketing of them in the U.K. The parent company employs economists at its head office in New York and in its affiliated companies around the world, using them in a variety of ways. Some are engaged in national income forecasting; some forecast broad magnitudes such as the consumption of energy and its division by fuels; others make estimates of the future demand for individual oil products and the Esso group's share of this demand; others analyse competitive energy industries; others are planners of one sort or another—looking at the broad directions in which the company's business should develop in the long term future or working on the short term planning of some part of company operations; others advise on help to formulate price decisions; and other economists assist in the management of the company's finances.

Obviously, none of these areas is the exclusive preserve of the economist—except perhaps in national income forecasting, which seems so esoteric to most people in business that business economists have so far contrived to keep a near-monopoly of it. In the others, economics is just one of the business skills which is found to be useful, though certainly one of the more important.

In Esso Petroleum, as in other affiliates in the group, economics graduates work in all these fields, using their economic knowledge to varying degrees. This chapter, however, is confined to examining only that group of people whose function it is to work as full time professional economists—the Economics Division of Corporate Planning Department.

Before dealing specifically with Economics Division it is best to explain very briefly how it fits into the Corporate Planning Department. This Department was established under its present name in 1963, though it took over many of the functions and the staff of a department called Co-ordination and Economics which had been in existence for many years before that. The main change which took place in 1963 was that CPD was given certain planning responsibilities which C & E had not had. CPD is a central staff department, with an establishment of over 20 people—fairly large for a department of this nature. Its Manager is one of the company's senior executives, who reports direct to the Board, and under him are three Divisional Heads. The Planning Division co-ordinates the company's long term objectives and plans; Mathematics Division consists of a group of professional mathematicians who work on new applications of mathematics to business (particularly forecasting and model building). The other Division is Economics with which this chapter is concerned.

The Economics Division and its Recruitment Policies

The size of Economics Division has varied but essentially it is a group of half-a-dozen people who provide the central expertise in economic affairs which the company feels it requires. All its present members are graduates in economics, some with considerable business experience and others recently graduated.

Whether to take people straight from university or to recruit only those with several years' business experience is one of the problems which faces anyone trying to run an economics department, and it is perhaps worth saying a few words about this.

The recent graduate has many advantages. With him or her one can be sure (assuming a good degree) that one is introducing a person who has been immersed in up-to-date academic thought and is therefore likely to bring in new ideas. The drawback is that the recent graduate has to go through a fairly lengthy adjustment process—at least a year and usually longer— before he can make any appreciable contribution to the company. This is a period which can often be disheartening for the new entrant and time-consuming for those who are training him. The underlying problem is that almost invariably the economics graduate believes that he has *something* useful to contribute to the firm without being quite sure what it is. After all, the economics he has learned is mostly about business and how it behaves, so it is natural to believe that he is one up on graduates in other disciplines. But the economics graduate, like anyone else, has to find out a good deal about what the firm does before he can begin to contribute usefully to it. Moreover, he has to adjust to the business world after being in an environment which is not generally sympathetic towards business. The gulf between academic and business economists in this country is far greater than it should be. Some universities nowadays encourage their good graduates to go into industry, some arranging for them to have working assignments with firms during their second long vacation, so they can get some idea of what it is like to work as an economist in business. But many universities are not really interested in business as an outlet for their best economists and some, unfortunately, do not provide the kind of training in statistics and quantitative economics which is so essential if an economist is to succeed in the business world.

This is not to suggest that firms are blameless. On their side, they often appear unsure what to do with economists—who seem a bit long-haired and possibly rather Left Wing—and may therefore leave them largely to their own devices. Eventually, therefore, both the young economist and the firm may become disillusioned. In Economics Division there has been a conscious policy of trying to help the recent graduate during this dangerous first year or so in order to avoid the disenchantment which can so easily set in.

The more experienced business economist, if one chooses well, should not pose these sorts of problems, though even he will find it takes a long time to immerse himself in the work of the company. However, there is an economic problem in choosing between the new graduate and the experienced man:

is the extra output of the economics group as a whole (in terms of the additional work done by the experienced man compared with the recent graduate, plus the smaller amount of other people's output lost because of time taken up in training) worth the extra amount one has to pay him?

In Economics Division there has been no set policy of taking either recent graduates or more experienced business economists. An attempt has been made to keep both types in the Division in the hope of getting an interesting and useful mixture of the different qualities which each possesses.

The Work of Economics Division

As with many economics departments the work of Economics Division is a little difficult to describe and classify since it is so varied—partly because there is a tendency to regard an economics department as a repository for any jobs which other people in a firm cannot do or are unwilling to do! It is best to discourage the idea that one's department is a dumping-ground for unwanted jobs; nevertheless, it has to be recognised that a firm needs someone to deal with tasks which do not fit neatly into its corporate organisation, and that economists can often do these kinds of things well.

(i) *The business environment*

Making allowances for these taxonomic problems, perhaps the best way to regard Economics Division is as a link between the normal business of the company and certain aspects of the outside which may affect that normal business. It is convenient to draw a distinction between a company's business environment and the decisions it takes within that environment. For example, a company is on the whole free to take decisions about what to invest, where to invest it, how much labour to employ, how to price its products and how much to pay its employees (though less so than it used to be). But all these decisions are taken within the framework of a particular business environment and the company's degrees of freedom will be a function of such things as the kind of economic policy the government is pursuing, the government's energy policy (in the case of an oil company or any other firm in the energy market), the actions of its competitors, and many other variables. In other words, there are a lot of things (which we can call the 'environment' for short) over which the individual firm has little or no direct control but which may significantly affect its development—and these things have increased in number over the last few years with the growth of government intervention in business. This distinction between the environment on the one hand, and the normal business operations of the firm on the other, is obviously rather woolly but it is a very useful one in practice.

Economics Division, then, is mainly concerned with looking at Esso's business environment, and in this it is different from most other parts of the firm which are principally engaged in conducting an efficient oil business within that environment. However, just examining the environment is in itself a useless occupation; the examination has to be translated into practical terms which the non-economist within the firm can understand. To illustrate, it is no use employing a man to make national income forecasts and then simply announcing that real GNP will rise by (say) 3 per cent. next year and explaining how all the expenditure components will change. Quite rightly, a firm's management wants to know what this strange fact is likely to mean in more down-to-earth terms. For example, what are the chances of a balance of payments crisis? If there is such a crisis, what are the alternative ways in which this might be dealt with and which are the most likely to be applied? Is taxation on the firm's products likely to be increased? Will credit be tightened? What is the final effect on sales likely to be?

This example of national income forecasting is put forward as rather an extreme illustration because national income is a difficult concept even for economists and it is no use expecting one's management to be able to understand it and its implications. They know the Law of Comparative Costs and the principle of division of labour and they concentrate on the things in which they have the greatest comparative advantage, employing specialists to do other things for them. It is worthwhile for a firm to employ a given person (even an economist!)

only if his work makes someone, somewhere come to a better decision than he would otherwise have done. Obvious as this may seem, business economists have before now lost sight of this important principle, and found their departments moving out on a limb, becoming more like branches of research institutions, making little or no contribution to the more efficient operation of the firm.

(ii) *Forecasting the business environment*

Since Economics Division is so concerned with Esso's business environment, a large part of its work consists of forecasting. The aim is to provide a picture of the firm's future environment and to draw out the major implications leaving other people within the company to fill in the details. Forecasting is an essential prerequisite to planning and the Division's objective is to provide the broad framework within which planning can take place so that better decisions will be made than if this framework had not existed. The environmental forecasts described below are the starting point for the company's forecasting and planning work and they constitute an integral part of Esso's planning cycle.

Our main forecasting efforts are centred around a simple model of how Esso fits into the economy and the energy market in this country. Simplifying, it is assumed that there are three (interdependent) environments which need to be analysed if useful forecasts are to be made. First, there is the U.K. economy, which obviously influences, and is influenced by, the development of the company. Second, there is the energy market (the total amount of energy consumed and its division between fuels), changes in which appear to affect the company rather more directly than movements in the economy as a whole, though in reality what happens in the energy market is often related closely to what happens in the economy. Finally, there is the oil market, which is the environment most obviously associated with the company.

In Economics Division, the first step in the forecasting process is to make national income forecasts—usually for seven or eight years ahead, though occasionally for a longer period. One apparently easy way of doing this would be to take or to adapt forecasts made by someone else—for example, the very professional and explicit short term economic forecasts made by the National Institute of Economic and Social Research could be used for estimating a year or so ahead. In Economics Division, however, it has been decided for several reasons that it is worth the time of one man to concentrate on making economic forecasts, making as much use as possible of sources such as the National Institute's *Economic Review*. For one thing, there are no authoritative long term economic forecasts published in this country, so that for the long term there is no alternative to doing it yourself (or going to an economic consulting firm). Then there is the point that in using a forecast it is important to know just what assumptions have been used in it and what the margin of error is likely to be; this is not easy when using someone else's forecast. It is also useful to be able to forecast variables in which you are interested but which others are not prepared to forecast. For example, we believe it to be vital to feed into one's national income forecast a forecast of the effect of government economic policy—a sort of 'before and after' exercise in which you start by estimating what would happen if the government did nothing, assess what the government is likely to do in these circumstances and then feed in the effect. A final reason for doing our own forecasts is that experience has shown that the Economics Division's national income forecasts have, over the years, been somewhat nearer the mark than possible alternatives open to us, partly because we have attempted to include this estimate of the impact of government policy.

This economic forecast then becomes a basis for other forecasting and planning work. A number of useful things can be derived at this stage—for example, the way in which the government is likely to deal with whatever short term economic situation is developing will already have been assessed and this needs to be looked at in more detail to see how this is likely to affect the company and whether there are any steps which can be taken to minimise the impact. Similarly, some useful conclusions about taxation policy in the longer term—both in general and as it may affect oil products—may be derived from the long term forecast. Some further comments will be made later on the conclusions which can be drawn from national income forecasts.

At the same time, the national income forecast is one of the essential components in forecasting demand for energy. Economics Division's approach to forecasting total energy demand is to split fuel consumption into a number of sectors which are economically meaningful and statistics for which are published. Total energy demand in each sector is then forecast by means of a simple quantitative model which relates energy to some relevant economic variables. In the domestic market, for example, consumption of fuel and light per head is treated as a function of real personal disposable income per head, temperature, and the ratio of an index of domestic fuel prices to an index of all consumer prices (with the elasticities generally being obtained by multiple regression analysis of past statistics), and the results are checked against estimates of the numbers of appliances using various fuels and their average consumption. Different variables are used in the models of fuel consumption in other energy sectors (e.g. industry, transport, offices and shops) but the principle used is the same—to construct a simple quantitative forecasting basis so that the assumptions which have been used in the forecast are made quite clear, enabling one to learn from experience by checking forecasts against what actually happens. In this way, if the forecast differs from the actual, as it generally will, the use of explicit assumptions gives one a reasonable chance of finding out why.

In practice there are, of course, many more problems in forecasting total energy than this brief, simplified description would suggest. One of the difficulties which most energy forecasters encounter is to find units in which to add up different forms of energy. Or possibly one should just not try to do this kind of addition. But this is not the place to go into these practical difficulties.

Having forecast total energy demand in each sector, our next step is to divide these demands between fuels—oil, coal, gas and electricity. On the whole, this is done by assuming that relative prices are the main determinant of any fuel's share of any sector and deriving estimates of price elasticities from past statistical data wherever possible, though this cannot be done if there have been no appreciable price changes in the past. If regression coefficients cannot be determined by analysis of the past, the only thing to do is to use one's judgement about what the price elasticity is likely to be; then at least an explicit assumption has been used and this can be checked against future experience. In some parts of the energy market other factors besides price may need to be taken into account; in some there seems to be evidence to suggest that technological changes (which may themselves have been the results of price changes) have been the major influence on the shares of the market held by different fuels. One other very important constraint which has to be kept in mind throughout this process of forecasting how total energy demand will be divided between fuels is government fuel policy and transport policy, since there is a considerable degree of government intervention both in the general fuel market and in transport. Economics Division makes assumptions about what these policies will be in the future, ensuring that its forecasts are consistent with the assumptions made and exploring the effects of varying those assumptions.

Economics Division's forecast of total energy demand and its division by fuels and by sector is checked against periodic studies of competitive energy industries which the Division makes. The competitive strength of each industry is examined and forecasts of output, financial position and prices are made. These studies are made in considerable detail; it is sufficient to say here that one of their main functions is to provide a valuable assessment of the strength of competition as well as serving to check energy forecasts made by other means. Periodic detailed studies of the transport market are also made; this is a market with its own special characteristics and one which is of considerable importance to the company.

The final stage in the Economics Division forecasting process is to examine the third environment—the oil market—and it is at this point that the Division's work merges most obviously with other parts of the company which are concerned with the business of operating within this market. From its analysis of the energy market, the Division has already arrived at forecasts of oil consumption by broad sectors—how much will be used in

F

transport, in domestic heating, in various industrial groups and so on. However, to be useful in sales forecasting these broad estimates need to be converted into estimates of the demand for individual products of the sort sold by the oil industry and produced at its refineries—fuel oil, petrol, diesel fuel, petroleum gases, etc. Moreover, this forecast of the demand for different oil products needs to be made for a few years ahead by months within each year, so that an analysis of seasonal variation has to be made and the effect of temperature fluctuations has to be assessed. Once this has been done, the result is a detailed analysis of how the oil market may look stretching some years into the future. This is then used by the Marketing Department in forecasting in detail Esso's own share of this oil market. These Esso sales estimates then become the basis for plans for supplying crude oil to refineries, for capital investment and for manpower plans. In this way, the environmental forecast is linked in to the detailed operations of the company.

One further thought is appropriate to finish off this rather simplified exposition of the forecasting process. This is that Economics Division's view of forecasting is one of (we hope!) healthy scepticism without going so far as disbelief. Many people, even some professional forecasters, have rather curious ideas on the purpose of forecasting, apparently thinking that it means making precise estimates of what will happen in the future (as though they were clairvoyants). We see this quite differently. Obviously no one knows what will happen in the future because the future is inherently uncertain. But the purpose of forecasting is simply, by approaching the subject of one's forecast methodically and scientifically, to reduce this uncertainty about the future. This implies, of course, that a range of values should normally be associated with the variable which is being forecast and that the forecast should be made in terms of probabilities. Too many figures can, however, be extremely confusing to management and the Division therefore adopts the principle of forecasting what it believes to be most probable, at the same time indicating to what extent and for what reasons actual experience might differ from this most probable forecast.

(iii) *Drawing conclusions from environmental forecasts*

This forecast of the business environment forms the basis of most of the work which Economics Division does. However, this does not mean that the group is entirely occupied in making such forecasts. In fact, a considerable part of the Division's time is taken up by drawing conclusions from them.

One of the most important of these conclusions is the sales forecast, with which we were mainly concerned in the previous section of this chapter, but there are others. In very general terms, what the environmental forecast does is to place the economist in a position to give the kinds of economic advice which he ought to be able to give; it places his company in the context of the external forces which are likely to shape its future and it allows him to comment on what those forces are and what their impact is likely to be. Without such a forecast it is virtually impossible to give useful economic advice: the economist is reduced to the position of, at best, an assiduous reader of the newspapers who can provide a general intelligence service for his management.

The kinds of subjects on which Economics Division expects to give advice—either because it is asked or because it simply offers advice without being asked—are so varied as to be difficult to set down in a short space. Some have already been touched on. The main ones are:

General economic affairs. The need to keep a watch on the government's short term economic policy (which in this country is largely governed by the balance of payments) has been mentioned. If one can assess both the developing economic situation and the government's likely general re-action to it one can then examine in more detail what government policy is likely to be—is it likely to raise taxes on oil products? What are the chances of corporation tax being increased? Will interest rates rise? Will it take direct action against a balance of payments deficit? and so on. On longer term affairs, one problem which has faced business economists in recent years has been to advise their managements on whether or not the Neddy and National Plan growth targets were likely to be achieved. On none of these matters can adequate advice be given unless it is backed up by national income forecasts of one's own.

Energy matters. The oil industry in this country has to be closely concerned with what happens in the other fuel industries—coal, electricity and gas—with which it is competing and with the government's fuel policy. Economists in the oil industry therefore need to understand how these industries operate and what their future prospects are (especially how their prices are likely to move). One of their most essential tasks is to try to understand and to forecast changes in government fuel policy. None of these things can be done efficiently without the benefit of the kinds of energy forecasts and studies of competitive energy industries which were described earlier.

The above examples assume that one has to take the environment as given, which is an assumption which should not be made lightly. As well as acting passively, explaining to one's management what factors in the business environment are likely to affect the firm in the future so that the firm can adjust to those factors, it may also be possible to try to *change* that environment. This is particularly true of government policy; the natural development of this in most fields is simply a series of responses to changing circumstances which, seen as a whole, may have no inherent logic. This applies to fuel policy in this country, which has arisen from a collection of *ad hoc* adjustments to particular problems made at various times in the past. In these circumstances, it is up to economists in the oil industry to make their views known both privately to the government, and publicly by making proposals for alternative systems which they believe would serve the economy better.

Some Conclusions

This chapter has necessarily been wide-ranging but there is one thread of argument, which runs throughout, which is perhaps worth emphasising at the end. This is that it is very easy for an economist or an economics department to become over-academic and isolated from the rest of the firm in which he works. The way to overcome this is to have a clear idea of those things which the business economist can do which are of relevance to his firm, to concentrate on those things (whether they are the kinds of activities described in this chapter or others) and to be able to explain their impact to people who are not economists. The business economist then becomes, as he should be, a professional man doing a specialised job which is an integral part of his company's operations.

4

The Economist in an International Corporation in the Primary Metals Industry

by J. A. CLAY

The writer is Economic Adviser to the Rio Tinto-Zinc Corporation Limited, a London-based international corporation, co-ordinating the activities of a number of companies, both in the U.K. and overseas. The principal members of the group are in Australia, Canada and Africa and are engaged in developing mining and related industrial operations, the main products being lead and zinc, iron, special steels, aluminium and copper. The principal overseas companies are largely independent within their national grouping; in other countries they are less so, but all co-ordinate with London the planning of their existing operations and the development of their new projects.

Forecasting Prices

The group is intimately concerned with international metal markets and with overseas finance. The main tasks of the economic adviser are the forecasting of metal and mineral prices, assessment of exchange rates, environmental studies of the U.K. and of other economies which have bearing on the company's policy. Forecasting of metal and mineral prices is undertaken for different periods ahead, (i) for the rest of each current year (for monthly reporting of results), (ii) for the following year for the financial plan which is prepared by all overseas centres and by the British industrial group in September and October each year, (iii) for the five year period in connection with the five year profit and cash forecasts (prepared the same way), and (iv) for periods from twelve to fifteen years in association with new project feasibility studies. These price forecasts are submitted to the Board for approval and used throughout the Group.

Annual Forecasts

Of these four forecasts, evaluation of price developments in the current year (i.e. for the remaining months of the year) is mostly a matter of market-place appreciation. Some influences can be quantified, such as stock levels, deliveries, orders and so on, but there is no scientific way of assessing what are often the more powerful political influences, such as wars and rumours of war, changes of governments, fear of U.S. stockpile releases, and strikes for industrial or political reasons. Some of these unquantifiable factors influence the flow of metal supplies round the world, others affect not so much the consumption of metal by fabricating industries as the demand, which can fluctuate widely and rapidly according to changing assessments of what stocks should be held at any time. Thus part of the economist's data in making a price assessment over the next few months is simply the range of views held by buyers on desirable stock levels at each stage of processing. Moreover these views often change rapidly. On a rising market buyers find that they cannot go wrong by buying further and further ahead, especially if there is any degree of restraint on price rises by producers concerned with the long term position of the metal. When suddenly supplies become adequate, and are seen to be adequate, buyers finding themselves overstocked according to their new assessment at once switch to living from hand to mouth and orders then fall away rapidly.

The timing of these turning points is very difficult to forecast, because they depend upon a general awareness by many people of a market situation and the technique of making these short term assessments is to obtain market views, together with the reasoning (if explicit) behind them, and also such other data on stocks, deliveries, iron curtain trade, etc., as one can, and then in the light of all this to make such guesses as are necessary to complete the picture.

Experience in appreciating short term situations often merges imperceptibly into a market 'hunch', which the economist is seldom close enough to the market to acquire; it also leads market men to take the view that since rational assessment of such short term situations is possible only to a limited extent, the same is also true of longer term forecasting when a 'hunch' nearly always proves unfounded. The short term exercises therefore endeavour to take a view which is neither optimistic nor pessimistic, since the former is dangerous in exaggerating total profit estimates and the latter makes the attainment of targets by constituent plants or mines too easy.

In this forward assessment as well as in other exercises, reliable information and statistics are indispensable and it is worth mentioning here that the collection of information and figures centres on a library which receives all relevant periodicals and publications. Press summaries are compiled each day and each week providing a very brief note on each item of interest to the Group serving not only the Economic Department's requirements but also disseminating information round the Group, cutting down at the same time the internal circulation of periodicals which so soon become out of date.

Following Year Forecasts

The 'next year' price forecasts involving all influences—market, political and economic—are the most difficult. Cyclical economic trends of the kind which produce balance of payments crises for Chancellors have to be considered, as well as market trends having their origin in production and stock situations. One has sometimes to decide how quickly a pending excess of production will make itself felt or be offset by other factors, or for example how long a de-stocking movement will continue. Sometimes a movement has long been foreseen but has failed, for some reason, to start; an example of this was the rise in the price of tin which began in 1963, and the break in copper prices in mid-1966. In all these cases the assessment of timing is very difficult since a strike or political disturbance can delay by many months what is in the end inevitable.

There are no subtle techniques which could improve these

forecasts; what is necessary is painstaking investigation of all current data and the analysis of very short term trends before attempting to weigh up the factors that have to be estimated. The developments that must be taken into account include the free world levels of output, the net balance of trade with iron curtain countries, as well as consumption trends for the major uses in the main geographical areas.

Five Year Forecasts

The five year price forecasts are based on much more sophisticated methods and techniques. Stock situations and other short term influences can reasonably be ignored, though the general economic measures of governments (often showing a cycle of two to four years) have to be brought in. Consumption trends become more important, demand elasticities for particular uses are investigated and elasticities of substitution introduced. The correlation of demand with another explanatory variable, for example gross domestic product or steel consumption, can look attractive, but it is of little use unless the explanatory variable can itself be satisfactorily forecast. (Who today would not regret such an exercise which in 1965 had used National Plan forecasts for gross domestic product?) While correlation of demand with the price of the metal, either current or lagged, is also used the results have been disappointing. Although some relationship does exist, in the case of most metals it does not appear to be simple enough to be usable. Simple trends against time if used cautiously over a long period of fifty years or so do in some cases offer much more useful results. On the production side, plans are usually known five years ahead, though delays are possible.

Twelve–Fifteen Year Forecasts

Lastly there are the long term forecasts, say twelve to fifteen years, for feasibility studies of new projects. The main complication here is that the supply side becomes much harder to predict as it involves estimating how fast new mineral deposits will be discovered. This however can be attempted on the basis of past experience but it brings up acutely the problem of producers' costs. These are not published by many companies and have to be studied with the aid of mining experts. On the demand side many intriguing problems present themselves such as the ten-year stagnation in U.S. copper demand which ended in 1962; this could be satisfactorily explained but the subsequent rate of growth is hard to assess and to extrapolate, especially in 1966 when the domestic price was held down by Government action so far below the world price. Who would not buy copper at 36 cents when the rest of the world is paying over 50 cents? Such inevitably short term situations make the work of the long term forecaster very hard. In general a fairly conservative long term estimate is arrived at with the object of neither discouraging the development of a viable mine nor of encouraging one which will turn out to be a sub-marginal mine when it opens, perhaps at a time of weak prices with all its short term debt still to be paid off.

In these forecasts one also has to deal with the problem of inflation. There is no steady rising trend in the prices of most metals to which one can draw attention in order to warn management against the risks of inflation. The price of copper for example fluctuated as usual in the ten years up to the end of 1963, but it ended where it began—at the same level. No doubt the influence of inflation was present but it cannot be isolated from other factors like substitution or any other market influences. There is nothing obvious to be gained by relating metal prices to general wholesale or retail prices, or in dividing the one into the other to get a 'real' trend.

For this reason with a fifteen year forecast for feasibility studies, which tend to base capital estimates on current quotations, it is preferable not to attempt to include the effect of inflation on operating costs and thus to work in today's values and to assume that inflation of costs and prices will cancel out. To draw attention to other price possibilities, however, we also make feasibility calculations based on one or two other prices close to our estimated price. This approach has the merit of showing how sensitive a new project would be to changes in price. In practice such sensitivity varies greatly.

It is worth mentioning briefly that the current level of prices at any time exerts a positively hypnoic effect on anyone concerned with the results, but not the task, of forecasting these prices. If lead and zinc are over £100 and copper over £350 then nothing in the world seems more natural than that they should stay there for ever. It is useless to point out that in the decade before the boom in prices which began in 1963, the average price (i.e. average of monthly averages) was £84 for lead, £81 for zinc and £255 for copper. The slowly rising trend of wages in most countries is no help to the argument that metal prices must inevitably rise in the future since there is a good deal of evidence to suggest that labour productivity is rising at about the same rate, i.e. that unit labour costs are roughly static. (This is probably not true of the Zambian copperbelt today and the consequences of this may have important implications.) One should also add that when prices are at depressed levels, it is just as difficult to persuade people that they will not necessarily stay there. Nothing for example could offer such a blank outlook as did refined lead in 1962.

Forecasting Exchange Rates

Another forecasting area of direct relevance and importance to international corporations is concerned with exchange rates. In an international organisation there are many problems concerning the effect of varying patterns of multiple devaluations upon the Group's structure of loans and debt, as well as receipts and payments of all kinds. This is not a matter of deciding at what moment, for example, sterling is in danger of devaluation and then hastily recommending certain actions in the light of the probable effect of such devaluation. By then it is too late to take any action not only because markets are likely to be too sensitive, but much more because a large company would not wish to add to the country's difficulties by selling sterling short, and thus helping to precipitate the very thing which it may be the Government's policy to avert. The writer would comment in passing that the boards of companies with which he has been connected have been far more concerned about the country's welfare than many politicians, or indeed economists outside industry, seem ready to believe.

One, is, of course, always concerned with the chances of devaluation in any country in which the Group operates, but frequent studies are required to assess the effects of a possible devaluation of one or more currencies upon a particular project where it operates, where it draws most of its fixed-interest capital, where its main shareholders reside, and where most of its sales are likely to go. The golden rule in a project with highly geared financing, supported by a long term sales contract (the typical case of our Group), is that the proceeds of the main sales contracts should be expressed in the same currency as the fixed interest debt. This is the case, for example, with our Hamersley iron ore contract with Japan. This is viewing devaluation from the point of view of preserving the value of profits or of assets and being able to meet liabilities. There is also the direct effect on prices. Market prices, if truly international, can probably be expected to remain unaffected in terms of the currencies which are not devalued. If there are no international market prices then an attempt may have to be made to escalate a long term contract price in terms of those costs which are expected to change as a result of devaluation, using official indices of wages, raw material prices, etc., exactly as one might attempt in the case of a metal price (other than those with international markets) to counteract the expected effects of inflation. There are many difficulties, however, in such arrangements, in finding suitable indices, in dealing with the residual profit and depreciation element and so on. The most satisfactory arrangement is when capital costs are a very high proportion of total costs so that a fixed long term price does not constitute too heavy a devaluation risk.

Market Research

Another type of work is concerned with industrial market research. At any one time the Group is investigating a wide variety of possible projects in different parts of the world. Sometimes the investigation is done entirely by the local company, at other times it is carried out jointly in conjunction with London, and when there is no local representation at all studies must be undertaken entirely from London. Such research usually proceeds in a number of stages, starting with a brief report on the product and possible markets for it together with notes on local conditions right up to a full feasibility and marketing study, covering all facets of the project. In between these there may be a series of progressively fuller reports as the project looks more and more interesting. This type of work varies greatly; sometimes the object is to find out existing and potential users of a material which does not enter into any regular market at all; sometimes there are local markets but not much of the material enters international trade. Sometimes grades and qualities differ sufficiently to make separate markets for each; sometimes there are substitutes linked with different processes, e.g. rutile and ilmenite with the two processes for making T_1O_2 for paint; sometimes there are linked materials as in the case of the three fertilizers elements in compound fertilizers (apart from the market for each which to some extent can be considered on its own).

There are occasions where outside consultants or indeed the Group's own firm of consultants are called in, for example where the market is so badly documented that field work is necessary to obtain information direct from users, or where in the final study particular techniques can be used with advantage which cannot easily be supplied from within the company. Sometimes a combination of outside and inside work is the answer where an elaborate market study is required to determine such things as the form in which the product is to be marketed, the various transport alternatives, the scale of operations as well as the most promising market areas. Finally under this heading, there are longer term research studies on the problems of diversification, i.e. of what industries to get involved with and of how far to integrate forward from any particular raw material. There are many interesting lines of enquiry, often extending into the general field of management as well as of economics.

Environmental Studies

This brings us to environmental studies—economic studies of the U.K. and overseas countries in which the Group is operating or planning to operate. This kind of study is a necessary background to current operations, providing forewarning of likely government measures arising from economic plans or other lines of policy, and also from crises due to balance of payments and other difficulties. In the U.K. at present there are two general areas where Government actions must be forecast or the results of declared policy deduced. First there are credit moves and tax changes affecting interest rates, methods of borrowing, dividend policy, and also indirectly the whole range of demand for the Group's products which are in our case raw materials for manufacture or immediate fabrication. Secondly, there are Government moves stemming directly from the balance of payments position, that is the restriction or relaxation of overseas investment (investment either by equity or loans or locally generated profits), of other international transfers, of tariffs, of aid, and of plans to proceed or otherwise into the Common Market and to threaten dissolution or otherwise of the so-called Sterling Area.

All these problems arise in varying forms also in foreign countries and mainly require short term general economic evaluation. In the U.K. there are many useful aids compared with the position twenty years ago, for example the *National Institute Economic Review* and the *London and Cambridge Economic Bulletin* and certain publications for foreign countries, which are now available. These greatly assist the work of the business economist, although he may not always agree with the general conclusions drawn.

In countries where such publications are not adequate more extensive studies are required. The writer has found that providing sufficient previous study is made and lists prepared of persons to be contacted such as economists in industry and in universities, central and commercial bankers, industrialists, journalists, etc., then a general economic report on the manufacturing and financial structure of an unfamiliar country with an assessment of current Government economic policy and the trend of productivity, inflation and the balance of payments can be produced after a visit of a fortnight or, in the case of a country with a particularly difficult language like Japanese, three weeks. This may sound superficial and even presumptuous but one finds in practice that a four or five weeks visit leads to a blurring of the image, as it were, so that if three weeks is to be exceeded then three or four months is the alternative or perhaps a repeat visit of a fortnight after an interval of a few months.

Such studies in connection with long term planning are

another matter. Having decided that a country new to the Group provides as far as can be seen a reasonable environment for future investment, one then has to live with it. It is extremely difficult to disengage five years later and go elsewhere, but it is also true that one cannot forecast the economic, let alone political, climate of the country for very long. On the other hand a Group can hedge its risk by spreading its investments over a number of countries (although even this does not cover the risk that a British Government will penalise investment in *every* overseas country).

These then are the kind of problems which occupy the writer and interest him most. Others of course come his way, some of them because there is no other obvious person to whom to refer them, or none with an adequate library conveniently at hand.

5

Economics and Market Research in the Rover Company

by Graham Bannock

I. Introduction

The Company's Size and Products

The Rover Company manufactures passenger cars, four-wheel drive vehicles, military vehicles, and gas turbine engines. In addition to Alvis with whom Rover merged in 1965, the Group includes Rover Gas Turbines Limited and has seven wholly owned subsidiaries or major interests in countries overseas, including sales companies in the United States and Germany and manufacturing/assembly plants in Australia, South Africa and Spain. Annual Group turnover is currently in excess of £70 million on a capital employed of about £25 million. The Group employs some 16,000 persons in the United Kingdom. Over half of vehicle production is sent overseas to almost every country in the world, the largest market accounting for 13 per cent of total exports, the second largest only 6 per cent.*

Management System

The Company has been expanding rapidly—vehicle sales have increased by an average of 15 per cent per annum during the last four years. With the introduction of the Rover 2000 in 1962, the character of its passenger cars has changed and cars also now contribute a bigger proportion of total turnover than they did previously. The rate of growth and the pace of innovation that has accompanied it has been reflected in changes in the management structure, including an expansion in the role

* Since this article was written, the Rover Company has merged with the Leyland Corporation.

G

of the economics and market research function. The Company has always had what might be described as an 'organic', rather than a 'mechanical' management system, that is to say the Board of Directors have set out to create a company environment in which the management system develops autonomously to meet changing situations rather than to impose a system designed to meet these changes. Day to day operations are, of course, decentralised, but the distinction between staff and line operations is not hard and fast. Policy making is naturally centralised, but there is a relatively high degree of participation in policy making by line managers and among senior specialist personnel who are, like the Directors, also involved at least to some extent, in line functions. This 'organic' system of management is flexible in its adaptation to change. It also promotes happy and satisfying working relationships among the staff to the extent that the organisation adapts, as far as possible, to the character and interests of its members. It further ensures that policy decisions are made under the influence of practical considerations. This management system, a natural one for small firms, is, perhaps, uncommon in larger ones but happens to be in accord with the theories of organic-adaptive management structure recently developed by behavioural scientists in the United States.* The system appears to have evolved spontaneously out of the traditions of the Company and the reaction of the senior management, as individuals, to external forces of change. Such a system is obviously more suited to cope with the formation of tactical rather than strategic policies but there have been compensating developments in the organisation to meet this weakness which is, in any event, less serious in a company with such a strong product tradition and sense of purpose as the Rover Company. These traditions are strong enough to provide a framework of constraints on the expediency of tactical decisions. The role of economics and market research in the developing organisation to meet the problems of major product policy decisions is given great emphasis in the following account of the department's functions. This has been done because it is in this field that the department's role is developing

* For a summary and further references see *Changing Organisations*—Warren G. Bennis, McGraw Hill, 1966.

most at the present time. The emphasis on product policy in the exposition is not intended to suggest that the other roles referred to are unimportant or to exaggerate the department's role in product policy making. Nor is it suggested that the general approach to economics and market research work set out in this highly individual account would necessarily be appropriate for other companies.

Economics and Market Research

The Market Research Department in the Rover Company is part of the Sales Division. It is split into three sections— Statistics and Market Analysis, Economics and Forecasting and Market Intelligence. The head of the last three of these sections is *primus inter pares* for administrative purposes, although all three section heads report functionally to the Company Economist. He, in his turn, is responsible to the Sales Director for the administration of the Department although to the Managing Director in his personal capacity as Company Economist. The advantage of this arrangement which is, of course, at variance with the 'mechanistic' management theory, is that the Market Research Department is supervised by the person in the organisation most technically competent to do so whilst the Sales Director retains control of an essentially Sales (in the wider sense of marketing function). At the same time, the Economist, whose prime role is in company planning, has influence over much of the compilation and analysis of information that he needs and which experience shows is inseparable at this level from the process of interpretation. At the same time the Economist retains an involvement in the day to day operations of the firm without having a major vested interest in a single division of the Company.

II. The Scope of Economics and Market Research Work

The Business Economist

The precise definition of the role of any business economist in terms of the academic definitions of the scope of economics is fraught with difficulties and is not attempted here.

Economists are what economists do. An economist is someone who is trained in the science of resource allocation. But resource

allocation is too broad a subject to define the role of the economist in the individual firm since, fundamentally, the allocation
of resources is the central problem of all company managers.

Strictly speaking a business economist *as such* can, in the
author's view, only be involved, passively, in supplying Management with economic information and interpretation, or
actively, in company planning. The former role is likely to be
challenging only in the very largest companies while the latter
is still organised on a functional basis in very few companies in
the United Kingdom. Company planning lays down the guide-
lines for strategic (and occasionally tactical) choices about the
firm's resource allocations to meet market conditions. In this
way it necessarily and naturally involves close association, as a
discipline, with market research which establishes what the
market conditions actually are. The fact that market research
and economic research are, for good reasons, often carried out
in the same department, as they are in the Rover Company,
should not confuse the functional distinction between them.

Economics, Market Research and the Marketing Concept*

The role of both economics and market research are being
much affected by the increasing adoption of the marketing
point of view in business organisation. The concept of marketing
is simply the notion that the firm's activities in producing goods
and placing them in the hands of consumers should be looked
at as a whole and with prior emphasis on the consumer rather
than on the technical problems of production or design. This
concept is naturally sympathetic to the economist who regards
the consumer's wishes, as expressed in the price mechanism, as
the basic determinant of the whole organisation of production.
This concept of marketing as applied to business organisation
merely reflects a change in emphasis from product and production orientation to consumer and market orientation. This change
of emphasis can be seen as a natural consequence of an achievement of a high standard of living where basic wants are easily

* This section, the following section and that beginning on page 102 are largely
based on an address given by the Author to the Industrial Section of the Market
Research Society, London, on the 29 March, 1966.

satisfied and the technical problems of production and distribution have become less pressing. Looked at in this way, the reason for the source of the marketing concept in the United States, and its greater progress in the United Kingdom in light consumer products than in heavy capital goods, can be more easily understood. The motor industry in this country, which is now approaching maturity in the economic sense, is rapidly becoming more and more marketing conscious. In this, it is, of course, somewhat behind the light consumer goods industries.

The implications of the marketing concept for market research are obvious; if consumer wants are to be given greater emphasis then greater attention must be given to finding out the nature of them. Not only does market research have a more important part to play but, because of its extension into new fields such as product policy and distribution, it is important that it should be more closely integrated with the main executive functions of the firm. The implications for economic research are a little less obvious. If the priorities of the firm's activities are turned upside down and the problems of consumer wants, sales and distribution become more important relative to those of design and production, then the problem of resource allocation becomes more difficult and their rational solution requires the quantification of many judgements that hitherto might have been left explicit.

Market Research in the Motor Industry

Compared with British industry generally, the motor industry has always been relatively very market research conscious. There are a number of reasons for this: the industry's volatility, the long development periods required for new products, a high degree of competition and, probably most important, extensive American influence on the industry's structure and methods of working.

The 'Big Five' motor companies all have upwards of thirty persons engaged in the preparation and analysis of statistics, market research and related functions and so do most of the main suppliers to the industry, as well as some of the specialist manufacturing companies. There are, however, enormous differences between the 'Big Five' in the organisation of marketing research, the type of research done and its influence on marketing policy as well as the amount of resources devoted to it.

All companies compile statistical records of their own sales performance and that of their competitors, carry out analysis of these records and report on their market shares, the relative efficiency of their retail outlets, trends in demand, etc. They also all prepare short and long term sales forecasts and provide an intelligence service on such matters as competitors' prices and specifications, tariff rates, economic conditions, etc.

There are, of course, differences in the relative importance of these functions and in the degree of sophistication of the methods used, especially in sales forecasting. The really striking differences in the extent and character of marketing research among the motor manufacturers, however, arise from the extent to which they have embraced the marketing concept, that is, the extent to which research is integrated with product policy, sales policy, and financial control. In short, these differences depend upon the extent to which firms are product orientated or market orientated. In this respect there is a fairly clear cut distinction between the American owned companies and the rest of the industry.

The American-owned companies tend to devote more resources to marketing research, especially in research involving direct or indirect contact with the consumer. The results of market research in these companies have a substantial influence on product planning and sales policy. The American companies also employ economics as a co-ordinating discipline, particularly in long term planning and in investment project appraisal, as a function distinct from marketing research.

The motor industry produces both consumer durables—cars, and capital goods—commercial vehicles, tractors, industrial engines and so on. Since at least 40 per cent. of the industry's car production is bought by firms and most of its commercial vehicles, the motor industry can clearly be classed as a producer of industrial, rather than consumer, goods. Market research in the motor industry is as much industrial as consumer research, therefore, and this, together with a relatively ample availability of statistics, is reflected in the considerable emphasis given to desk as against field research.

The Rover Company

The Rover Company's economic and market research activities cover all the fields surveyed above. *The Statistics and Market Analysis Section* maintains records of the Company's orders, production and dispatches. It also analyses and records returns from home and overseas distributors of retail sales and stocks and maintains records of the Company's retail prices and discounts. These functions are all concerned with the Company's own statistics, most of which have to be worked-up from raw data. There are also parallel functions concerned with industry and competitors' statistics. There is no shortage of material about the world motor industry. It is usual for companies to exchange statistics with their competitors at home, and less frequently overseas also, both bilaterally and through trade associations. Most countries publish official statistical data of motor vehicle production and registrations and a mass of technical and commercial information appears in the world press. Except for attempts to fill gaps arising mainly from the specialised nature of the Company's interests, the work of the Section is mainly that of sifting and recording rather than obtaining statistical information. The Section issues a minimum of regular reports, it being policy to monitor and report on trends and exceptions rather than to issue streams of information that have to be digested elsewhere. In addition to motor vehicle statistics the Section maintains records of tariffs, taxes, economic and other factors affecting the sale of vehicles.

The Market Intelligence Section is concerned mainly with product policy. Its functions fall into three main groups. Firstly, the Section provides a recording and information service on technical matters similar to that provided by the Market Analysis Section on commercial matters. Detailed and up to date records are kept of the performance, running costs and specifications of the Company's vehicles and their competitors. The Section also studies, from a statistical point of view, trends in engine size, the demand for automatic transmissions and other technical matters that are susceptible to quantitative analysis. Secondly, vehicles are loaned to, and borrowed from, competitors and assessments made of them from a customer, that is to say, non-technical, standpoint. Field research is carried out among retailers, customers, and potential customers to establish customers' views about vehicles and other market characteristics. This particular work has been singled out for more detailed discussion. The third function of the Section is to advise on short term product policy, i.e. 'face-lifts', optional extras, and long term new model policies.

The Economic and Forecasting Section assists the Sales division in the preparation of its short term sales forecasts for production and sales planning purposes. It does this by supplying the Division with total market forecasts on the principle that market share forecasts can only be made by the selling department and can only be made accurately on the basis of the fullest information on the total market. Similar assistance, but with greater involvement, is given for Financial Year forecasts. The Section also prepares long term total market and company sales forecasts for periods of three, five and ten years ahead for all programmed and tentative forward vehicle projects, monitors them and reviews them on a regular basis. It does this in conjunction with the Market Intelligence Section and the rest of the Sales Division. Unlike short term forecasts, the Market Research Department and not the Sales Division as a whole is the initiating source of long term sales forecasts. Such forecasts, of course, have to be adopted by the Sales Division and the Main Board of Directors before they form the basis for investment programmes (see page 102 below).

The Economics and Forecasting Section carries out economic research as a basis for its forecasts and into other matters on which it is called upon to advise, e.g. on pricing policy. It also assists in liaisons with the D.E.A., N.E.D.C., and The Society of Motor Manufacturers and Traders Limited.

Although called upon to give information, advice and help on financial problems of all kinds, e.g. in analysing competitors' company accounts*, the Economics Department in the Rover Company has no direct responsibilities in the financial field. It does not assess investment projects as it does in some American owned companies in the industry, although the Accounts De-

---

* These studies are sometimes part of more general studies of competitors' whole corporate strategy which have proved useful in company planning.

partment rely upon the Economics Department for sales volume estimates and other elements of its regular five year cash flow forecasts and project assessments. This is justified on the grounds already touched upon on page 92 above, that Economics is a market-orientated discipline and that in a company with a management structure of the type of the Rover Company the principal functional link should be with a marketing rather than with a financial function. In industry in general, economists are increasingly concerned with the detailed analysis and appraisal of investment projects from a purely financial standpoint. Although this trend in the emphasis of economists' work still has a long way to go, it is quite conceivable that, ultimately, it will be partially reversed as accountancy practice absorbs the economists' new techniques for investment appraisal.

III. Techniques and Problems

A. General

The toolbox of techniques in frequent use in the Economics and Market Research Department is quite small. Virtually the whole corpus of economic theory provides a useful framework for the assimilation and understanding of the mass of institutional knowledge that has been built up about the motor industry and its environment. Simple econometric techniques are used for forecasts as a basis for the exercise of judgement and, of course, statistical methods are used to analyse data as in trend fitting or in establishing seasonal patterns and in obtaining data, as in sample surveys. These econometric statistical techniques and their relevance to problems in the motor industry have already been described in a book in which the author collaborated.* In general, the techniques actually employed involve little mathematical sophistication. In short term sales forecasting, for example, the use of exponential smoothing has not, so far, been practicable because of physical problems of obtaining and computerising the processing of the necessary data and, in the case of Land Rovers, by certain technical problems, e.g. that posed by the relative importance of 'lumpy' fleet orders. In long term forecasting the development of sophisticated technique has, paradoxically enough, been frustrated by shortage

* *Business Economics and Statistics* A. J. Merret & G. Bannock, Hutchinson, 1962.

of time. The development of sophisticated models for total market forecasting is very time consuming because of the large number of variables (some of which are difficult to quantify) that have to be taken into account. When balanced against their likely contribution to accuracy as alternatives to, for example, greater refinements of market share forecasting, model building of this kind is in the Company's experience quite uneconomic for a company of its size.

This view that the individual firm should not devote too much of its economics department's resources to original total market forecasting work extends to more general 'conjunctural' economic forecasting also. It is just not possible for the company economist to devote time to really detailed forecasts of G.N.P. or to all the factors affecting, for example, the balance of payments or the level of world trade. All he can do is to follow the discussion in the press and elsewhere and adopt with a greater or lesser degree of modification, depending upon the importance of the issue to the company and the amount of research involved, the analyses and forecasts of such independent bodies as the N.I.E.S.R. or the O.E.C.D.

B. Planning for new products

For a relatively small firm, the economics department can make a contribution of much greater importance in the areas of market share and product policy than in those of total market forecasting or environmental forecasting. Since the smaller firm in an industry is, as a matter of policy, seeking for market opportunities which will not bring it into *direct* competition with the large manufacturers, it follows that the size or even growth of the total market is of less importance to it than it is to the bigger firms. The market share of the larger companies is remarkably stable—that of smaller ones much less so, so that the effect of relatively large errors in forecasting the total market can be swamped by errors in forecasting market shares. The smaller company is often exclusively interested in sub-sections or classes of the market which often grow or contract at different rates from the market as a whole and sometimes in quite different directions. Much interesting work has been carried out into this subject by the company. Class movements within the total market are affected by spontaneous changes in tastes and by the marketing policies of manufacturers as well as economic factors. The most fruitful areas of economic research in this field have been into income distribution and international and inter-regional comparisons.

The Rover 2000 has enabled the Rover company to more than double its share of the United Kingdom car market between 1962 and 1966. The biggest change in market share amongst the 'Big Five' motor manufacturers over this period, the effects of mergers apart, was probably not more than fifteen per cent. and the total market grew by only twenty-five per cent. over this period. Such a big change in market share is possible because a small firm is in a position to create a sub-section of the market by taking a small amount of business from all of its competitors over a wide range of price groups. Market creation, i.e. creating a new class within a total, is only rarely possible for a large manufacturer who requires a substantial volume for every new model and does, in any event, call forth a rapid response from its competitors whose sales must be significantly affected by the introduction of a large volume new model for which they have no direct counterpart. Ford's Mustang in the United States and General Motor's response is an example of such a case.

The great scope for increasing market share through the introduction of new products, and the correspondingly heavy penalties for failure, explain the importance which the Rover Company attaches to the role of the economics and market research department in product planning and market share forecasting.

The most illuminating way of illustrating this role would be to give case studies. Unfortunately this is not possible since such case studies would be of great value to the company's competitors and for this reason cannot be disclosed. This is particularly true of work that has been carried out into the markets for specialised vehicles such as that for the Land Rover where very little published information is available at all. The following general account of some of the problems of desk and field research, with particular reference to passenger cars may, however, illustrate some of the issues involved.

The product planner never has a clean sheet of paper to work on. He has to work within a number of parameters set by past decisions. Finally, there are those set by Company policy, in the case of the Rover Company to design vehicles with export and domestic requirements equally in mind, and, as far as cars are concerned, to build quality cars costing over £1,000. Secondly, parameters are set by past decisions on engine policy, machine tool and factory layouts and so on. These factors are not permanent, but it is usual for them to have major importance within the planning period for any new model. For this reason all the decisions taken in these, or similar respects, with particular new models in view must be preceded by a thorough examination of the extent to which they will limit product policy in the future. Thirdly, parameters are set by the nature of the Company's selling and service organisation and its public image.

Essential groundwork for product planning is a monitoring process for the market as a whole. The Company's and its competitors' sales figures must be continuously analysed, changes in trend examined and underlying causes exposed. The failure of a new model or the decline in sales of an existing one should throw up clues for the development of successful ventures. In this sense the world market can be seen as a laboratory in which each failure and success provides material for an understanding of market requirements and how they are changing.

The concept of a new model usually comes from Senior management, or the Engineering Department, or it may be generated directly by the monitoring process described above. If it is seen to be consistent with the technical and commercial parameters of the firm, then the rough characteristics of the model are sketched out by Engineering Department. Approximate costings and capital requirement estimates are then made by the Value Analysis and Estimating Department while the Market Research Department develops probable sales volume figures. This is essentially an exercise in desk research. For radically new products simple guides are not available, but for most new products some guide can usually be found in the past experience of the Company or its competitors. Inter-firm comparisons are thus of great value and so are comparisons between motor markets in countries at different stages of development.

Although much more of an art than a science, a rigorous framework of analysis is necessary for new model sales forecasting. A complete dynamic model of the Company's vehicle market is built up which includes total market estimates for five and ten years ahead and estimates of the Company's practicable market share objectives on the bais of existing product programmes.

Estimates for new models must clearly distinguish between *total sales volumes and incremental volumes*, that is the amounts by which introduction of the new model will raise the Company's total sales. *Substitutional sales volumes*, that is the losses of sales that will be sustained by other models already in the product programme and the effects of these on product mix and hence upon profitability, must be assessed. The source of incremental sales in terms of the Company's competitors must be defined. The discipline of being forced to guess exactly where market share will suffer should act as a brake upon excessive optimism and a knowledge of what the Company or its more successful competitors have been able to do in the past should prevent pessimism.

Accounts Department then roughly assess the financial viability of the project, in terms of these estimates, of the effects on sales volume, product mix, and capital requirements. This assessment may suggest that the price could be reduced, or that some reduction in cost is necessary to give a larger margin of profitability. In these cases the sales estimates, of both the specification and sales estimates, are reassessed.

If it is decided at this stage that the project has a reasonable chance of success then engineering development proceeds. When the major technical problems have been solved and a prototype built and assessed, a major feasibility study can be carried out on the basis of more precise information on costs and prices. When this study has been completed the final decision to go ahead with the project is taken. This decision is taken by the adoption, by the Main Board, of a brochure containing details of the capital expenditure involved and the market assessment which underlies the model programme. When this decision has been taken only the broad outlines of the model are still irrevocably fixed. Detailed market research proceeds, and this research, reflecting not only deeper knowledge of the market

but the changes that are occurring in the market over the conception and gestation period of the model, interacts cumulatively
with technical research and the collective experience of senior
management to produce the new model in its final form.

Some remarks about the role of field, as opposed to desk,
research are necessary. Mr. Alec Issigonis is said to have re-
marked that the motor manufacturer has to tell his customers
what they want. This would, at first sight, appear to imply that
market research can make no contribution to product policy
and might, indeed, be taken as an expression of an excessively
product-orientated approach to design. However, the converse
is certainly not true; the motor manufacturer cannot ask his
customers what they want and then design and produce it—if
he did the results would almost certainly be disastrous.

In the first place, most car buyers' views about cars are
limited by their own immediate experience of motor cars, often
of only one make. They may not know, even by current standards, how their car compares in all respects with others. In
asking for more acceleration, for example, they may not know
that their present car compares unfavourably in other, and
what might prove to them equally important respects—in ride
or handling—with its competitors. Nor are buyers always aware
of the extent to which their requirements for power and economy, compactness and space, reliability and cost, may conflict.
Most important, buyers cannot be aware of the technical progress that research makes possible and which may change
completely the characteristics of the cars they may wish to buy.
The inability of car buyers to say what they will buy is, of
course, increased by the lead time on product development
which may be from two to five years, or even more for a
revolutionary new model.

A further and equally important reason why you cannot
simply ask car buyers what they want, and then give it to them,
is that they do not necessarily know what they want. Motor
cars are chosen not only as a means of transport but are, like
clothes, chosen as an expression of personality. In this respect
there are subconscious motivations. The Rover Company has
asked carefully selected samples of car owners to rate, in order
of importance, the factors governing their choice of car—price,

reliability, economy, performance, comfort, appearance, safety and so on. The order given is often inconsistent with the object-ively verifiable characteristics of the car they own. Probe questions and image comparison invariably reveal that styling and social factors are much more important in determining a choice of car than people know or will say.

What has been said about motor cars is, of course, true to a lesser extent of other consumer durables and to a much smaller, but surprisingly significant, extent of capital goods too. The point that you cannot evolve a product policy by simply asking people what they want has been emphasised because it is a common misapprehension that this is, in fact, what is done, or what should be done in market research in the motor industry. In practice consumer research is carried out with three principal objects. Firstly, to find out as much as possible about the buyers of particular classes of cars—their ages, occupations, media exposure, and other socio-economic characteristics and the type of use to which they put their cars. Knowledge of this kind is primarily helpful, in conjunction with analysis of statistics of sales, in making *deductions* about customer requirements. The second object of consumer research is to find out about customers' experience with the company's existing products and this is helpful in developing new products as well as current ones. The third object of consumer research is to analyse customer motiva-tions and to assess Company and product images. This informa-tion is primarily helpful in advertising policy, but in revealing what is important to customers, it can have a great bearing on product policy too.

One of the advantages of consumer research in the motor industry is that most people are pleased to discuss cars and particularly with the manufacturer of the car they own. The Rover Company have found that carefully planned postal surveys among its owners, for example, regularly produce re-sponse rates of seventy per cent., much of non-response being due to change of address, or reasons other than unwillingness to reply. It is also found that such postal surveys provide very useful information on the characteristics of our customers— their ages, occupations, the kind of driving they do, the adver-tising media they see, and useful criticism that is helpful in developing models in current production as well as future models. Checks with sales and other statistics and sample surveys have shown that, probably because of high response rates, the results are very representative and accurate. The great advantage of postal surveys, of course, is their low cost. Even allowing for a pilot interview survey, which is considered essential to help frame the questions correctly, the total cost for a sample of 3,000 owners does not exceed £500.

A flow of information about the Company's customers comes from pre-paid questionnaire cards sent out with every new vehicle. The response rate here is much lower—about twenty per cent. of domestic customers and only five per cent of export customers. Export market research, of course, presents many problems. The Rover Company exports half of its output to 170 countries and the assessment and reconciliation of the often conflicting requirements of these markets is one of the most difficult aspects of product policy research. Considerable assistance is given in obtaining information of these requirements by overseas subsidiaries and distributors.

To obtain information about potential customers, as opposed to existing owners, sample surveys are carried out. These have been primarily motivation surveys designed to establish the image of the Company's products and those of its competitors, why people buy them and why they do not buy them.

It would be foolish to exaggerate the role of market research in new product development—especially for major new products. The basic conception of a great motor car is usually the work of a very small group of people, although they will depend upon a large organisation to give it birth. Highly successful cars are not conceived by committees of market researchers, even though their work has an important role to play in their development. This role, as far as product policy is concerned, and as the Rover Company see it, is mainly to ensure that creative engineering is done with a full knowledge of what is going on in the market. At a later stage market research has a much more central role in fixing prices, production planning and marketing policy generally.

6

Investment Decisions in a Large International Company

by ALLEN SYKES

Background

RTZ—the Rio Tinto-Zinc Corporation Limited—is a large international company whose main interests are in the development of natural resources, principally mining, and related industrial processes. The company is a major producer of uranium, nuclear products, lead and zinc, and a substantial producer of iron ore products, copper, bauxite, alumina and aluminium, and stainless steel. It also has substantial smelting, chemical and fertilizer interest, and the management responsibility for the recently sanctioned thousand-million dollar Churchill Falls hydro-electric project in Labrador. Finally, in addition to a host of minor activities, the company has large investment holdings including the Zambian copper companies, British Titan Products, and B.P. The total capital employed in the company at the end of 1965 was £125m, which put it twelfth in size in the 1966 British ranking list of the *Times Review of Industry and Technology*. The geographical split of assets in descending order of importance was:

Australia	36·4%
North America	26·2%
United Kingdom	18·7%
South Africa	12·3%
Zambia	4·3%
Europe	1·6%
Rhodesia	0·5%

Third party sales in 1965 were £116m, pre-tax operating profit

H

£10·8m, gross investment income £7·4m, and tax £5·5m. Net profit after tax attributable to RTZ shareholders was £9·5m on shareholders' funds of £88·7m. Capital expenditure is a figure with marked fluctuations from year to year, but in 1965, the additions were at an all time high of £64·6m. The RTZ Group's capital outlays are such that they could not be financed from internal resources alone even if that were thought desirable. It is the practice to seek international partners for most sizeable projects and to raise substantial amounts of debt finance. At the end of 1965 long term debts and advances comprised 46 per cent of capital employed.

To enable its various subsidiaries to undertake large diverse capital projects, often simultaneously, it is necessary to give the U.K. parent company the task of co-ordination. The RTZ parent company is thus responsible for advising on the acceptability of all significant capital projects and for advising on appropriate ways of raising the necessary finance, although proceeding with the project, and guaranteeing the finance remains the responsibility of the subsidiaries concerned. To assist the nine executive directors of the parent company to carry out these financial and economic tasks is a 25 strong corporate planning department known as the 'Group Planning Department' headed by one of the executive directors. The department is split into various sections including a General Commercial Section, the Economic Adviser's Section (responsible for metals and commodity price forecasting, the state of the economies of the countries of interest to the Group, monetary and balance of payments problems, etc.), a General Budgeting Section (for collating, checking and analysing forward budgets), and a Financial Section. The Financial Section has seven financial analysts, all graduates. While degree subjects range from economics and science to law and mathematics, all members have a thorough grounding in micro-economics and accounting.

Tasks

The Financial Section has three main tasks: analysing all major capital projects, investigating all the factors affecting profit optimisation including risk and uncertainty, and helping on

financing plans. While these problems are the particular responsibility of the Financial Section of the Group Planning
Department in practice the work is done in close co-operation
with other sections and, of course, with other major departments
that are involved, such as Technical and Tax Departments. A
considerable amount of the work is done in conjunction with
operational research specialists.

The parent company is informed of the details of all proposed
capital projects of any consequence as well as all proposed
acquisitions and new ventures even where small sums may be
involved. The Financial Section has the formal responsibility
for doing the analytical and investigatory work on these projects
and new ventures.

The brief is interpreted widely. Long term leasing arrangements which involve no capital expenditure would be considered by the Section if the amount involved is significant. The
same applies to long term contracts for sales, services, etc. In
short, the responsibility is to consider all significant outlays of
money whatever form they take.

Although the RTZ Group has very large annual capital
expenditures, the greater part of such expenditure occurs in
single very large-scale new projects. Typically, the Group will
be bringing to fruition one large-scale international project
costing £30m to £40m at the rate of one a year. Such projects
usually take several years to plan and something like 1½ to 3
years to construct. Usually several such projects are going forward simultaneously, but usually at different stages of development. It is the investigation and analysis of these projects which
forms the bulk of the work of the Financial Section.

Projects first come up at what is known as the 'preliminary
review' stage. A preliminary review seeks to answer the question
whether, on the preliminary data that is available on a project,
it looks to be of serious interest such that detailed marketing,
costing, and engineering work will be justified. The review
would normally include preliminary estimates of such factors
as the type of product, likely markets, minimum economic
production levels, capital and operating costs, transport costs,
availability of labour, housing, etc. It is intended to throw up
as early as possible which of these factors are critical to the

venture. The Financial Section will normally carry out an analysis of the data in the preliminary review to help to determine whether proceeding to the next stage is justified. Often it will become apparent at this stage that some particular factor, e.g. a minimum sales contract, is essential to the success of the venture. Particular attention can then be paid to this aspect at the next stage.

Once a project has passed the preliminary review stage, the next task is to prepare a detailed feasibility study. This will usually involve detailed engineering, costing, and marketing studies. Depending on the complexity of the project sometimes several feasibility studies may take place, each one more comprehensive than its predecessor. While the preparation of such feasibility studies is the responsibility of and is carried out by the subsidiary company concerned, the Financial Section, and indeed the whole of the Group Planning Department, will be working on the problems involved, making suggestions, and carrying out profitability calculations, often at the request of the subsidiary company concerned.

Before a project is finally sanctioned a definitive plan must be presented. The important point about this plan is that to the best of the Group's knowledge it should be the *optimum* plan from the viewpoint of maximising profits in the light of all the risks involved. This plan usually emerges as a result of the combined activities of the sponsoring company and the parent company. It is in the development of this plan that the Financial Section and indeed the whole of the Group Planning Department play a significant part. The actual techniques used are discussed below but in brief the aim is to investigate all the combinations of the different estimates of sales, capital and operating costs, taxes, tariffs, etc. It is not sufficient to produce a plan which will produce an acceptable level of profit. The idea is to produce the plan promising maximum profits: in short, the right project, at the right size, built in the right place, at the right time.

It is not possible to choose the optimum plan without reference to how the project is to be financed. As mentioned previously the RTZ Group raises substantial amounts of loan capital on international markets and usually goes into major ventures in the partnership of other international companies. To determine the optimum plan for the Group therefore requires detailed investigation of financing possibilities and the terms on which other companies may be allowed to participate in the equity of the project. The negotiation of loans and financing participation is co-ordinated by the RTZ parent company, and requires the quantification of a great many possibilities. It is this latter task which is the particular responsibility of the Financial Section plus the suggestion of alternative terms, counter-offers, etc.

Techniques employed

To carry out the above tasks adequately, it is necessary to have a working knowledge of micro-economics, management and financial accounting, and business finance.

The need for accounting knowledge should be obvious. Accounting is the language of business. Projects are typically put up in accounting language and when presentations are made to other companies, and to banks and other financial institutions, they are cast in an accounting form. The need for basic knowledge of business finance is also obvious. To some, however, the need for a working knowledge of micro-economics might not be so obvious. The choice of the optimum way to do something, however, is clearly the province of economics, and the guiding principle is that of opportunity cost.

One of the obvious uses of the opportunity cost principle is to determine what constitutes a minimum acceptable profitability. The RTZ basis for choosing this standard is the return which shareholders and lenders can get on comparable investments outside the company. To measure such returns adequately it is necessary to take account of the *timing* of capital outlays and profits. This leads inevitably to discounting methods. Full use is made of all the major discounting methods, in particular the calculation of DCF returns. At the staff level, particularly for optimisation studies, considerable use is also made of the net present value variant. For many projects, particularly those which make use of basic services such as electricity, much use is made of the annual capital charge variant. (This latter variant is particularly useful in calculating power costs in terms of kilowatt hours.)

So much for the methods of calculating profitability, the next point to consider is the measurement of risk and uncertainty. Even in the academic literatures the difficulties involved in this subject are far from resolved, hence the methods employed are necessarily in the experimental stage. But as a matter of routine the full range of permutations is calculated for all the major variables on a project, sales, capital and operating costs, economic life, etc. To enable this to be done cheaply and quickly, use is made of an advanced computer programme developed in conjunction with the company's operation research specialists. The need to look at a large number of variables is necessary for two reasons. First to highlight what constitutes the critical factors and therefore as an aid to assessing the risks on a project. This process goes under the name of sensitivity analysis. Second, it is necessary to look at his large number of variables in the interest of optimisation. If sole reliance were placed on hand calculations it is doubtful if some of the more implausible possibilities would be thoroughly investigated, yet occasionally it is just such apparently implausible possibilities which turn out to be of serious interest.

The next stage in analysing risk and uncertainty is to incorporate specific probability estimates into the calculations. This matter is under urgent investigation but has not yet reached the point where it can be incorporated into a formal system.

An Example of an Overseas Mining Project Evaluation

The process of investigating, analysing, and sanctioning a capital project is perhaps more easily appreciated if related to an example. Set out below is a fictitious case study incorporating some of the features of a typical project.

(i) Background

Batala is a small Atlantic island lying midway between the Bahamas and West Africa. The colony of a West European country, it was settled by European farmers in the seventeenth century and produces sugar, rum and coffee. As a result of mineral surveys commissioned by the colonial government a small but high grade iron ore deposit has been discovered. The deposit has been offered to RTZ for investigation on the basis that the company has two years to test and investigate the property and draw up a detailed project plan at its own expense. If RTZ elects to go ahead with the project the government wants a 20 per cent. equity interest, a 3 per cent. royalty on the F.O.B. value of sales, and at least half the annual output to be in the beneficiated form of oxide pellets or sponge iron. (These products involve processing iron ore to make a much higher grade product. The thought here is to increase export income, to promote industrialisation, and to increase employment.) If RTZ does not elect to go ahead with the project all results of surveying and planning are to be handed over free of charge to the colonial government.

(ii) *Preliminary Review*

The offer by the colonial government set out above would normally be subject to a preliminary review by the RTZ subsidiary concerned. If a project does not automatically fall within the sphere of interest of one of the subsidiaries it would normally be processed by the parent company: this procedure is assumed for the project considered here. A preliminary review by the parent company would involve several departments, including the Tax Department, the Technical Department, the Marketing Department, the Shipping Department, and the Group Planning Department. The object of the preliminary review would be to establish whether or not there was a prima facie case for taking up the offer. The Technical Department would examine the available drilling data to determine whether the ore was of a mineable grade, and whether reserves were sufficient to sustain an economical size operation. In the light of their investigations the Marketing Department would examine the feasibility of selling the likely range of output for the project and give some indications of prices. The Shipping Department would examine the existing harbour facilities on the island and any available information which might indicate the possibility of improving such facilities if desired.

It might well emerge at this stage that the likely price at which the iron ore could be sold would indicate a sea-freight such that only ships in excess of 40,000 tons could meet it. The Shipping Department would then have to say whether or not this was feasible with the present facilities, or at what cost could present facilities be altered to permit handling ships of the relevant size.

The Tax Department would examine the status of mining ventures for the island and any double tax agreements, etc. All these sources of information would be collated and analysed by the Group Planning Department and a preliminary review made to help the executive directors decide whether the offer could be accepted at all, and if so, whether any modifications were either necessary or desirable. In the case under considera-tion it might well emerge that the offer as it stood was unaccept-able unless RTZ was released of the obligation to beneficiate at least half annual output, undertaking merely to study the economic feasibility and desirability of so doing. Another point that might emerge at this stage would be that the island tax system did not cater for industrial or mining activities and special legislation might be called for to ensure reasonable treatment consistent with mining tax treatment in other countries.

In the light of the preliminary investigations by all the departments concerned, a preliminary survey would be pre-pared to show if the project was likely to be feasible. To do this a preliminary budget would be prepared by all the departments concerned to show the cost of a detailed investigation of the various matters which were their responsibility. On the basis of these estimated costs the Group Planning Department would calculate the preliminary economics of the project to determine if there was sufficient indication of profitability to make the feasibility investigation worthwhile, or what factors would need to be altered to make it worthwhile. From this exercise it could well emerge that the project was sufficiently attractive to war-rant investigation but only if RTZ were relieved of the obliga-tion to export any of the output in a beneficiated form and if the colonial government would give an undertaking to introduce taxation provisions suited to a mining venture comparable to those existing in other mining countries. These factors would be incorporated into a counter offer and, if accepted, RTZ would proceed with the detailed feasibility study.

(iii) *Feasibility Study*

The feasibility study of any project of consequence could well last several years and is unlikely to take less than six months, unless it becomes apparent at an early stage that it is not worth proceeding further with the project.

The starting point of the study would be the market analysis. Marketing experts would make a study of where the iron ore in both its natural and beneficiated form might be sold. In the case in question it is likely that Europe would be the most favourable, indeed perhaps the only likely market. The next step would be to contact the main consumers and to sound them out on quantities required, likely prices, and whether or not there was any possibility of a medium or long term contract.

While the marketing investigation was proceeding, or even before it commences, a full scale technical investigation would be mounted. Geologists would work out the drilling figures to date in greater detail and determine whether or not further drilling was required. Usually further drilling will be required and this will be carried out, after which the best methods of mining will be determined. This will, of course, depend upon the amount of ore, its location, whether or not the orebody is uniform, etc. At the end of these investigations the capital operating costs for the range of possible outlets of ore will be prepared. Harbour facilities will be investigated and the cost of any extensions, handling facilities, dredging, etc., will be investigated. A further matter to receive attention will be the availability of local labour both to help in construction and in operating the main and associated facilities. A full investigation will also be mounted regarding availability of water, power, housing, etc.

Tax matters will also receive full investigation and any special concessions required will be indicated.

On several occasions during the course of this study, the information made available on all the matters listed above will be drawn together and the preliminary economics re-investigated. It will usually become apparent that the economic output will come down to a clearly reasonable range of outputs, and that beneficiated products may seem to be quite uneconomic. The result of these intermediate calculations will determine the direction of subsequent investigations.

The profitability and optimisation studies made by Group Planning Department will involve calculating production and financial schedules for all the cases considered. Where these cases are sufficiently numerous use will be made of special comprehensive computer programmes entirely designed by RTZ staff. For each permutation there will be calculated the DCF returns on total and equity capital, and also net present values for total and equity capital (these latter being particularly useful to the analysts engaged in the optimisation work). This will be done for a range of assumed operational lives. There will also be calculated the annual debt service cover for all likely financing schemes and the breakeven periods necessary to recover debt capital plus full interest thereon. Also the breakeven periods on total capital will be calculated, with the minimum equity return requirement used to calculate 'interest' on the equity capital. The reasons for concentrating on the returns on total capital, as well as equity capital, are that an attractive return on equity capital is an insufficient basis for going ahead with a project unless the return on the total capital is also adequate. Only when a project passes the minimum requirements of return on total capital is the return on equity capital considered. In the calculation of breakeven or capital recovery periods for projects subject to a time risk, it is important to calculate the 'interest' cost of equity capital because only when all the capital has been recovered, plus the minimum return thereon, can the company be said to have broken even in any meaningful sense.

As the project nears the end of the feasibility study, the likely customers will have been identified and the likely quantities which could be sold. From this the likely capital costs of the project will be clear and hence the amount of finance which has to be provided. Preliminary talks will take place with financial institutions, so that the likely sources of finance will be identified.

The feasibility study will determine the optimum output (or range of output) and will show whether or not the project is sufficiently profitable for such an output. Then a decision can be taken to proceed with the project, providing sufficient contracts can be made and that the requisite financing is forthcoming. It may well be that insufficient finance is available for the size of operation which is most attractive. While an investigation would be made for alternative financing sources it could turn out that little or no further finance is forthcoming. In view of this it would have to be determined whether the project should be postponed or started on a smaller scale with the intention of expanding it when new funds are available.

When all these matters had been resolved, the company would reapproach the colonial government and negotiate the final terms for going ahead with the project. This might well involve a re-arrangement of equity participation, the size of related tax allowances, etc. Assuming all these matters are resolved satisfactorily, the company would then proceed to sign contracts, raise the finance, and complete the project, satisfied that all the relevant factors had received adequate consideration, and that profits had been optimised to the best of the company's ability.

7

The Economist in Distribution

by Jan de Somogyi

It is inevitable that all classifications have to be somewhat arti-
ficial and all generalisations a bit sweeping. Tasks performed
by economists differ widely between companies, even within the
same industry.

The frontier between manufacturing and distribution is an
arbitrary one; marketing is essentially a continuous process,
from the factory floor to the shop counter. Problems of distribution are as much of interest to the manufacturer as they are
to the retailer. As companies which employ business economists
tend to be large and their interests wide, an economist in retailing will frequently come across production problems.

Introduction

In general, the kind of contribution made by an economist will
first of all depend on the company climate in which he works.
Secondly, a great deal will depend on his own point of entry
within the company, and the extent to which he succeeds in
becoming a part of the organisation; without such integration
he can seldom make a really useful contribution.

I shall now try to describe my own work and functions along
these lines, and then try to isolate those features of my experience which I consider, in a wider sense, typical of a business
environment as opposed to a manufacturing industry. I shall
stress the type of economic problem which is characteristic of
distribution, and emphasise the type of approach which may
have a more general application outside my own company environment and indeed, outside retailing. Such generalisations

are useful only if they are based on a particular situation, which
I shall now outline.

The Company

Because of the remarkable consistency in its historical development and the continuity of its top management, Marks and
Spencer has evolved a coherent body of economic, marketing
and management theory for the use of its management and
staff at all levels. This business philosophy is based on six
principles:

1. to offer customers under the company's own brand name,
   'St Michael', a selective range of high quality, well-designed
   and attractive merchandise at reasonable prices;
2. to encourage suppliers to use the most modern and efficient
   techniques of production, dictated by the latest discoveries
   in science and technology;
3. with the co-operation of these suppliers, to enforce the highest standards of quality control;
4. to plan the expansion of the stores for the better display of a
   widening range of goods and for the convenience of the
   customers;
5. to simplify operating procedures so that the business is
   carried on in the most efficient manner; and
6. to foster good human relations with customers, suppliers,
   and staff.

Social and Economic Trends

For over half a century this well-defined business philosophy
has been developed and flexibly applied to the changing conditions in which Marks and Spencer has been trading. The
story of the business is that of a continuous up-grading of quality
in the merchandise and in the amenities in stores offered to
customers and staff.

   This trend has been parallel to the great social and economic
changes which have created an incomparably more prosperous
and more homogeneous society than that in 1884 when Michael
Marks opened his first Penny Stall in Leeds Market, or in 1926

when Marks and Spencer was made a public company, or even in 1954 when the country emerged from the period of war and post-war austerity. The company has not only benefited from these changes, but in some ways it has been in the vanguard of progress.

Theory and Practice

The growth of the business has thus been largely due to the Board's awareness of the changing economic and social environment and the ability to look and plan a long way ahead, while remaining sensitive to short-term economic fluctuations.

The inter-relationships between the environment and the company at both micro-economic and macro-economic levels have been under continuous scrutiny. The Chairman's Annual Statements, since Marks and Spencer became a public company, show this pre-occupation both with the economic environment within which the company has been trading and with the coherent body of business theory on which its growth has been built.

In both these areas, the late Lord Marks of Broughton was an acknowledged genius. With his brother-in-law, Lord Sieff, who is now the President of the company, he worked out a unique concept of business. Already in the thirties, Lord Sieff, himself an economist by training, drew on the company's experience in the public debate on Britain's long-term economic problems. He was already then interested in planning and founded P.E.P. The belief that the economics of the business and of the nation are closely related has always been firmly established at Marks and Spencer. The company's buying methods became a subject of a study by a team of civil servants—the first venture of its kind in this country.

Business Economist

I think it is important to stress that a professional economist has no monopoly and, indeed, it would be unfortunate if he had. In most large companies, there are people both on the Board and at other levels of management, who have intimate experience of economics, both theoretical and practical. It is one of the most important tasks of a professional economist to learn from this experience, to formalise it, to use it and to pass it to others. I have myself been exceedingly fortunate in my teachers and hope that I shall never lose the capacity to learn.

Human Factor

Retailing is a simple and personal business. The chain of production and distribution culminates in a personal situation at the counter where goods are sold. As compared with industry, success depends less on technical solutions and to a greater extent on the full understanding by the management, the staff, and not the least, the customer, of the role the business has chosen to play. This is a matter of clearly defined policies, of training and of human relations. It is in this area of human relations which is so often neglected or misunderstood in theoretical or applied economics, that a professional economist in distribution can make his own contribution.

The human factor should never be underestimated but in retailing it is of particular importance. At Marks and Spencer, human relations, good communications and good organisation have always received special attention. Growth of the business has always been considered in organic, that is human, terms.

Organic Growth

Long term thinking and planning are essential to economic growth. The development of merchandise must be parallel with the development of stores, and the recruitment, training and development of staff. Successful growth of the whole enterprise depends on all these processes moving in step, so that counters can be clothed, new space available to display the widening range of goods, and the continuity of experience preserved; without it nothing will succeed. The whole process must be orientated towards the customer and the experience gained on the shop floor passed back to the supplier.

The growth must be organic, not mechanical, depending on the co-operation between retailer and manufacturer, involving merchants, store management, technologists, designers, engineers, administrators and specialists of many kinds. The whole economic system thus created, its behaviour and its dynamism, must be properly understood. Many problems emerge, some small and some large, and they have to be tackled. A wide range of industries is involved, many raw materials, many scientific disciplines. The scope of economic research is very wide.

Marketing

The origin of Marks and Spencer's approach to marketing can be traced back to the time when goods were created to a penny price point, and later in the inter-war years within the 5s. ceiling. The usual marketing sequence was reversed so that it began with a price point and quality standard, based on customers' demand. In the traditional sequence of marketing, goods were made first, and the price emerged only after everyone involved in the process had added their margin. Economies resulting from efficient large scale production and distribution are passed on to the customer in lower prices and higher quality. Today, most of St. Michael goods are sold under 100s., but the principle remains.

The problem of achieving economies of scale in production, resulting from the use of better processes and equipment and from economies in distribution, through larger stores and better systems, are the constant pre-occupation of the management. The question of what constitutes better value and the customers' preferences between lower prices and higher quality are of paramount importance. Inevitably, the problem of inflation has occupied the key position in the post-war years, and the comparative movements of raw material prices are keenly studied.

Economist as a Member of the Team

It is evident that all these important problems could not be tackled by one, ten or even a hundred economists, but they must be dealt with as they arise by top management and by individual marketing teams. But an economist has a part to play and his work must mirror that of the management. Perhaps no

I

other person in the business, outside top management, has access
to an interest in such a wide range of company's activities.

If, however, top management is concerned with both thinking
and decision taking, the economist is concerned with what
I would call 'practical theory'. He must have his head in the
clouds but feet on the ground; even if he reports to the Chairman
and the Board he should also serve the whole of the management to acquire the practical view of the organisation and maintain intimate contacts with his 'staff' or 'line' colleagues. This
will prove a useful experience of the business which he can feed
into the main stream of his advisory work. This is a service to
the company, as it provides an additional channel of information, both up and down the line.

Economic Information Department

The economic department at Marks and Spencer provides the
information on the economic, social and political environment
of the business, as a background to decision taking. Its functions
include a monitoring service, an information service and an
advisory service which covers economics, statistics and communications.

The Economic Information Department was evolved in 1958
from the Economic Research Department and the Research
Co-ordination Department before that, with antecedents going
back for more than a quarter of a century. The re-organisation
in 1958 gave the work of the department greater immediacy and
brought it nearer to the centre of decision taking. It is a small,
compact department, working as a team and its economic
graduates have retail management experience.

The department has a modicum of routine functions arising from
the daily flow of information and otherwise operates selectively
with continuous re-appraisal of priorities. It is impossible to
cover comprehensively the whole range of the problems affecting the business, nor is this necessary. Economic planning and
long term thinking take place throughout the whole of the
organisation.

The department's main duty is to monitor and to provide an
early warning system. It facilitates, where required, surveys

conducted by other departments and carries out long term studies up to the point where they become 'live' and are taken over by operational departments. There are many problems which need consideration though some time will elapse before they can have a direct impact on the business. On the other hand, the department often gets called, in its information or advisory capacity, to report at short notice on a variety of urgent problems.

Priorities

It is typical of Marks and Spencer that even specialists like the economic department are completely integrated in the way of the business. Activities of an advisory service of this type, if successful, tend to snowball and Parkinson's Law must be resisted. By continually reviewing the priorities within set physical capabilities, it is possible to steer the work to the most promising channels, giving it the maximum of timeliness and relevance to the business.

Problems of storage of information are approached in the same spirit. Physical restriction is imposed on the storage space. It is better to do the job afresh than get bogged down in 'dead information'. It is preferable to get rid of the books and even re-purchase again, than to tie-up a lot of space and people in filing. Nothing is kept in drawers, and books are displayed on open shelves. The approach here is, quite rightly, the same as in stores. Stock must always be 'fresh' and the 'slow sellers' must be cleared.

The same criterion of selectivity is applied to internal communications. Writing is kept to the minimum and attention is paid to clear and logical presentation. Reports are written within the physical limitation of a given length. This is a good discipline which secures selectivity.

Interpretation

In spite of his complete integration within the business, the economist must cultivate a certain attitude of detachment to gain a perspective of the company in its economic and social environment. While he is expected to interpret the company's philosophy and principles within the business and for the out-side world, e.g. in helping with the preparation of policy docu-ments and speeches, he also has to provide for his Board and management his own interpretation of economic events and their impact on Marks and Spencer.

It is the confrontation of the two overlapping worlds which provides the opportunity for the most creative work. It is also here that the theory and discipline of economics are most useful, if tempered by intimate knowledge of the business. This is also the most demanding role in contrast to the purely technical functions of providing economic information or economic and marketing studies and analyses. It is these functions however which are the base of the pyramid of which the interpretative and advisory functions are the apex.

Monitoring Service

In a service department of this kind, it is important that there is a wide area of contact within the business and good lines of communication. As the organisation itself is never static the department cannot afford to stand still. Because of the speed and the flexibility required by a retail operation the monitoring service must be prompt. The raw materials for this operation are the teleprinter news service, daily press, journals and gov-ernment and other publications. Information is passed on, depending on its nature by means of press cuttings, photo copies, or by word of mouth.

A continuous spotlight is laid on the matters which are at that moment operational, for the executives who are responsible for them. This service is highly selective and the priorities and terms of reference shift from day to day. Yet, while due emphasis is given to matters of the moment, preferably anticipating the events, certain long term developments of importance to the business are kept in the forefront when the opportunity arises.

The service is individual so that those who 'hook in' to the information network receive an individual selection from the news, depending on their work and requirements. This may include extracts from the daily press, weeklies, monthlies and special reports. The top management and the executives concerned are notified of the press references to the company by 10.30 a.m. on the day these items are published. Other daily press-cuttings are sent out by noon, but important teleprinter news is dealt with as it arises.

As a by-product of the monitoring service a monthly *Press Review*, with a circulation of nearly 1,000 copies, is published as a means of information, stimulation, and training for management at head office and stores.

Enquiries

The Economic Information Department provides a focal point where information can be consulted and where advice on its interpretation, evaluation and amplification can be obtained. The department makes use of outside contacts: other economists, civil servants, libraries, research institutes and universities. The department deals with economic surveys originating from outside the business or passes them on to the people concerned within the company. A small library is maintained so that questions can be answered promptly and a variety of research conducted.

The matching of supply and demand for information is like merchandising; it depends on the knowledge of the customer and the familiarity with sources of supply. Information is valueless unless it is available when it is wanted.

Some questions require probably only little research in published economic statistics, some may involve discussions within the company or outside, and some may require very considerable thought and research. The subjects covered range over a wide area; retail sales, prices, production, information on companies, unemployment figures, population statistics, exports, government regulations, and many minor inquiries.

Marketing

It is a striking feature of retailing, as compared with manufacturing, that the policies of any individual large company, its outlets and its business approach are clearly visible and apparent. With self-selection or self-service and proportionate display, where space is allocated to goods according to their sales, a large retailer has few secrets. In fact, it is a matter of surprise to me how little this source of information is utilised in marketing and economic research. With this abundance of information freely available in every high street, retailers themselves tend to be very practical, and they cultivate a 'seeing eye',

There is a strong conviction in Marks and Spencer that sales will increase only where the merchandise and the price are right. It was Alfred Marshall who wrote of supply and demand as a pair of scissors, neither blade cutting on its own. This is very much the sentiment in the business and the emphasis is always on goods. Future success largely depends on past, present and future efforts, and it would be wrong to attach too much importance to statistical trends.

The share of the market in individual lines is nevertheless of interest. The estimates of national sales are particularly useful when entirely new lines are launched, though a good product will create its own market. If all is well, outside competitors should not even be in the running and the company's products will compete against each other for sales floor space. The whole store network, with the trial line system, is a laboratory for merchandise development, and provides a special kind of 'market research'.

Store Location

Academic literature, particularly in America, is full of store location case studies. On the other hand, there is no substitute for personal expertise and a visit on location provides, in many cases, most of the answers as to the potential of the site. A story is told of Gordon Selfridge, who himself studied shoppers, pedestrians and bus passengers in Oxford Street before building his department store there. This is now the prime location in the country and the neighbouring Marks and Spencer's 'Marble Arch' branch has one of the ten highest turnovers for any kind of retail outlet in the country.

Few store development decisions in this country are taken in isolation from the existing trading situation, as is the case in siting an entirely new shopping centre. Shops are therefore opened and developed in relation to the existing shops in the high street: large new shops in relation to the existing shopping centre; small shops and chains in the wake of the large ones which act as magnets to a shopper.

Systematic classifications of shopping centres, according to the ensemble of shops represented there, banks, cinemas, etc., are therefore of interest. Two studies have been published for the London area: one is an appendix to the Report of the Royal Commission on Local Government in Greater London 1957/60 (by W. I. Carruthers); the other by the Institute of British Geographers (by A. E. Smailes M.A., and G. Hartley B.SC., 1961). The ranking of shopping centres is based on the supply alone so that a declining or 'overshopped' street gets undeserved prominence. Fortunately this is immediately apparent to a store executive with experience. The Census of Population and the Census of Distribution provide a comprehensive, though infrequent, background of information, the latter now including sales figures for most shopping centres.

To provide a broad framework of national figures is useful, but it is important to follow the example of the weather forecaster who liked to sit next to the window. Many reports one comes across must have been written in the basement.

Store Development

There are three sources of economies of scale in retailing: vertical development (larger store) horizontal development (chains) and development of central functions (administration, ancillary services, buying and merchandise development). Frequently all these forms of development take place simultaneously.

Since the war, the store development programme of Marks and Spencer has been largely based on the expansion of existing stores. The economics of store development are not widely understood outside retailing nor the relation between the investment in retailing and productivity. Retailing is labour intensive and the most promising way to improve labour utilisation, i.e. increase sales per head, is to increase, where possible, the size of store. The relationship between the size of trading units and labour productivity can be linear—provided there is scope for development. Internal information on the performance of the stores, taken together with the information on the hinterland, provides all the elements for ranking priorities.

Forecasting and Economic Analysis

As compared with manufacturing, retailers are much more concerned with, and much more clearly affected by, short term trends. They have to react quickly to these, but if they are to be successful they must also subordinate these reactions to a long term policy of growth.

Unlike most manufacturers, retailers find that their own sales figures are among the most advanced forward economic indicators. Among official statistics only the note circulation figures (relevant for example at Christmas) and national savings figures appear weekly. This being so, an economist in retailing can usually get more out of a careful analysis of the company's own weekly sales than from national statistics.

A great deal of useful work can be done on time series, e.g. by a careful scrutiny of seasonal variations, evaluating social trends in shopping (bank holidays, etc.), and studying the influences of weather on sales. These seasonal co-efficients, based on weekly sales, can be developed into a delicate and sophisticated instrument for interpreting what is actually happening to sales at a given point of time. This is not always easy, particularly when the weather and economic factors coincide. At a forward position in time, a good assessment of the present situation is superior to a forecast based on 'stale' statistics.

To get further forward in time it is necessary, however, to make general assumptions about trends in purchasing power, retail prices and industrial earnings. These three factors dominate the scene, as far as the retailer is concerned, both directly, by affecting the basic pattern of sales, and indirectly, by bringing about deflationary action by the government. The official fiscal policy and economic policy must be studied so that the type of reaction can be anticipated. Changes in purchase tax, income tax, import surcharge, credit restrictions, etc., have varying effects on retailing, through incomes, through prices and by diverting spending from one type of goods to another;

the shift from hire purchase to cash and from durable goods to clothing and vice versa, are particularly important.

Retailing Today

The Retail Sales Index has at present a major shortcoming: it is based on the 'kind of business' classification which relates to the type of shop and not the type of merchandise sold. With the post-war revolution in retailing, larger stores and a more diversified catalogue, this kind of business classification is becoming obsolete.

The result of the type of store development in depth which I have already described, has been the emergence of large stores which offer a wide range of pre-packaged goods from large unpartitioned floors and rely on self-selection or self-service by their customers. With the growing size of individual outlets, a much wider range of goods is now being offered under one roof, and this is being helped by developments in packaging and food technology which facilitate the selling of different commodities, including food, in close proximity to each other.

A new class of stores has emerged which embraces e.g. variety stores, supermarkets and discount stores, as well as some large and more specialised stores such as ours. Many of them are links in the chains but some are independently owned. All these stores, in spite of the great difference in their marketing policies, have a great deal in common, though the Board of Trade statistics still divide them into butchers and bakers and candle-stick makers.

There is a pressing need for a new cross-classification based on the size of the store, to allow for the new large outlets which are often larger in terms of sales than traditional department stores. A rough breakdown of sales by groups of commodities would also be of great help.

Statistical Comparisons

The problem of classification in the Board of Trade statistics is made worse by the statutory secrecy concerning the allocation of any individual store group to any class. As this is not always obvious the statistics are sometimes difficult to relate to the reality of the high street. For instance, Marks and Spencer's sales, food and all, are included with the women's wear shops, and even some retailing textbooks draw wrong conclusions from the figures because people are not aware of this fact.

The commodity analysis in the Consumer Expenditure Tables is much more useful but the Central Statistical Office figures are still published only quarterly and at one point of time there is nearly six months' time lag. There is hope that this fault will be corrected. The relationship between personal incomes, domestic consumption and company sales is very useful as a framework for looking ahead, particularly if allowance is made for price changes. With a large company it is useful to consider the additional purchasing power and spending in absolute terms in addition to the general approach based on percentages.

The habit of comparing one's performance with that of a year ago is a deep seated one. The official statistics have now placed their emphasis on seasonally corrected, volume adjusted figures. Press comment on January sales may now state that they were up on December, seasonally corrected! Given the shortcomings in classification and the subjective element in seasonal corrections, the figures are far away from reality. Also, unfortunately, the reliability of the index of retail prices is open to some misgivings because of the rate of marketing innovation in some goods, and the large subjective element in finding substitutes.

Pragmatic Approach

Perhaps the greatest scope for statistical methods is in the evaluation of store figures and the results of 'experiments' for which a multiple organisation is singularly suited. This body of systematic self-knowledge is cumulative and provides a quantitative counterpart to the theory and philosophy of the business.

Retailing, because of the nature and speed of its operations, encourages a pragmatic, empirical approach. New ideas, new merchandise and new methods can be quickly evaluated by studying customers' reactions. This is in contrast to manufacturing where many years pass, particularly in heavy industries, before the results of the policies can be tested. In retailing, as in any other modern business, decisions depend on a quantitative assessment: of sales, costs, operational statistics etc. But this is not all. The favoured solution will have to fit in with the experience of the business, within the context of its overall strategy and, most of all, take into consideration the human angle—the customer, the supplier and the staff.

Business Philosophy

Because the economic department is in daily contact with both the directors and executives and is involved in a whole host of inquiries, a body of knowledge of the business and its environment is built up. It is also a function of the department to participate in professional conferences and meetings etc., so that close contact is maintained with current thinking in the country on economic, social and political problems.

The common feature of all these functions is the concern with the entire range of the company's activities, seen in the context of national life. The constant outward flow of information and the return flow of requests and inquiries, is the lifeblood of the department. By being in contact with a great many people, both outside and inside the business, the department strives to obtain an early knowledge of any new developments within or outside the company. The inquiries received are the barometer of the business.

At the apex of this pyramid of information and statistics, is the assistance given by the department to the members of the Board in connection with statements of the company's policy. The economist's contribution in these areas is mainly in the form of analytical exposition, clear thought and an element of detachment from the implementation of policy.

Conclusion

I have described the business environment within which the economic department operates at Marks and Spencer, its general functions and its approach to their fulfilment. Apart from the particularly strong 'personality' of Marks and Spencer, which pervades all the work, the way the department operates and the work it does is not always specifically related to retailing. In fact, as I have already said, the company's interests extend way beyond traditional shopkeeping. In any case, differences in the environment between retailing and manufacturing are more important than the differences in the content of work.

1. Retailing is an intensely *personal business*. It is a service industry which depends on satisfying the needs of the customers. The personal element, merchanting sense and intuition are strong, even where technologists are employed to translate these into concrete specifications. In retailing, or for that matter anywhere else, the human element must never be overlooked or under-estimated.

2. Retailing is a very *fast moving business* where quick response is particularly important. Because retail sales are the most advanced forward economic indicator, the retailer, unlike the manufacturer, finds most published statistics lagging behind his own sales. On the other hand, he is in the happy position of being able to find out what is happening by having a look for himself.

3. Retailing, because of the nature and speed of its operation, encourages a pragmatic, *empirical approach*. New ideas, new merchandise and new methods can be quickly evaluated by studying customers' reactions. By contrast some manufacturers may have to wait many years before the results can be tested. There is a greater premium on an up-to-date awareness of the trends and on the ability to draw sensible conclusions quickly from one's experience.

4. Retailing is a *simple business* and even with self-service it is *labour intensive*. The competitiveness of any organisation depends to a very large extent on its business philosophy and principles, as much as the competitiveness of a company in a technological industry depends on its technical superiority or manufacturing formula. The greatest asset of the retailer is through the goodwill of his public, the quality of his management and the kind of relationship he has with his suppliers. The price of success is continuous improvement and awareness of the changing trends.

8

The Economist in the City

by T. M. RYBCZYNSKI

The economist in the City is not a new figure. Long before they penetrated the industrial and commercial world, City institutions have counted economists as members of their fraternity and actively used their skills and abilities. Specialist economic departments have been in existence in the City for some decades and economic reviews and publications from the area around the Bank of England, raising matters of public interest and drawing a picture of the U.K. and world economy, have come to occupy an important place in the nation's commercial and intellectual life.

Indeed, it is no exaggeration to say that the City has been the one area of business with which economists have been intimately associated for many years. It has provided them with opportunities of contributing directly and indirectly to the formation and execution of policy of the various City organisations, of applying their ideas, of blending theory and practice together and learning how the intricate economic mechanism works. Distinguished and eminent economists as exemplified by Ricardo and Lord Keynes have spent a considerable part of their working lives in the Square Mile, to the advantage of the City, the organisation with which they had been associated, the economic strength of the nation and the development of economic thought.

At present the City accounts probably for up to ten per cent. of the non-university economists in the U.K., whose total number can be estimated at some 2,500. The former figure probably understates their numbers for in the City more so than in other walks of life those with economic training and experience tend to move at an earlier stage to the executive side of business and the demarcation lines between various skills and functions are not as tightly drawn as elsewhere. In addition employment of economic consultants in advisory and part time positions has been accepted in the City for a very long time. Those involved not infrequently after a while move to full time positions, whose economic content is very large.

Broadly speaking the financial institutions where economists are very strongly represented comprise banks, some insurance companies, brokers and those involved in the management of funds in one way or another. In addition, economists in the City are employed by a number of non-financial institutions such as shipping companies, international corporations and holding companies. The outstanding feature they all share with their colleagues in industry is their youth. Most of them fall into the twenty-five/thirty-five age bracket often including heads of departments set up only recently to provide services now considered indispensable.

Banks as a rule have separate economic departments whose size tends to vary according to the functions they undertake. This is also true of some of the insurance companies, while in brokers' offices and other organisations economists described as such tend to work with relatively few colleagues but are to a large extent engaged in duties where they combine their skills with others, as for example in investment and analysis. In addition it is common to find economists attached to other departments undertaking duties of a highly specific character.

The exact nature of the duties and responsibilities of City economists tends to vary both with the type of business their organisations carry on and the firm they work for. Nevertheless there is a certain common ground they all cover, which has been changing in some significant respects. The three main strands of work carried on by them comprise the provision of a comprehensive picture of the development of events outside the firm and its evaluation for the firm and its clients, production of publications containing general and specific information for external and internal purposes and finally close co-operation with management on the strategic and operational problems facing the firm.

Assessment of economic trends in the various sectors of the U.K. economy as well as the behaviour of the economy as a whole and of overseas countries has always been an important function undertaken by the economic departments of the banks. Some of that work has been available to the public at large in the regular publications which until not so long ago were one of the few well informed and reliable sources on which business and often official bodies could draw and use for policy formulation. These reviews, containing articles of general interest often contributed by outside economists, still play an important role. They are now supplemented by other publications written specially for clients and the general public providing up-to-date information on the position of the economy using principally official statistics but often supplemented by data collected by the banks themselves. Those engaged in the work are general economists who must have a first class understanding of the structure of the economy, the interdependence of its various sections and its relation to the world economy. They must also be capable of using and interpreting statistical techniques of an increasingly sophisticated type.

Alongside general publications there have emerged in recent years a number of special pamphlets and booklets of an informational character designed for the general public, and either prepared by economic departments or produced in co-operation with them. These tend to cover subjects such as the setting up of business abroad, foreign exchange regulations, Common Market, trading in Eastern Europe, etc., and are a small part of the comprehensive and increasingly complex informational and advisory services provided by the economic departments of the banks. Open to all their clients they are also used on a regular and *ad-hoc* basis by other departments of the banks. They cover a bewildering variety of problems from simple ones about the cost of short-term funds in certain countries abroad to detailed reports about the prospects and possibilities of the financing of specific industrial projects. Comparable to the intelligence services which the authorities have used for many years, they play an important part in the day-to-day operation of business.

Broad assessment of the economy, forecasting its future course and analysing and interpreting the implications of findings has also been one of the basic functions of the economists working with some insurance companies and brokers. This type of work has been closely connected with the evaluation of the conse-quences of trends for the stock market as a whole, as well as for specific industries and individual companies. It is closely connected with the work of another of the new professions, that of investment analysis, whose primary function is to evaluate the prospects and investment merits of individual stocks and shares as compared with others and in relation to prices as a whole.

The third main function performed by economists in the City has been that of liaison and co-operation with management. This advisory and co-ordinating function covers firstly assess-ment of the position of the firm in the industry and the economy and the broad lines of its development and secondly appraisal of the policies pursued or to be pursued for internal organisation and methods of working. To relate the firm to its environment, to present a picture of future trends, especially now that govern-ment policy and other external factors are so all-pervading in their influence, and to be able to quantify the results is some-thing for which economists, with their wide knowledge, analyti-cal abilities and numerical skills are eminently suited. For this purpose economic departments carry out special research pro-jects, commission them from outside consultants and organise special services that are indispensable for rational strategy and efficient day to day operation. It is only natural that this systematised knowledge be used for internal purposes of innova-tion and co-ordination in the world of finance in the same way that it is now used in industry. Now that the process of collecting, organising and purposefully using knowledge to attain well defined objectives is assuming an increasing importance, econo-mists in the City are becoming one of the main nerve centres, gathering the reflexes from the outside world and helping to translate these into the reactions necessary for the short term and long term prosperity and survival of the firm.

Within this broad framework there has been in the last few years a marked tendency for specialisation. Although in some ways special to the City, this trend has been noticeable within the whole field of business economics. At present four areas of specialisation, or perhaps special interest, can be distinguished in the City. They comprise general economist, banking economist, corporate finance economist and investment economist. General economist, as described earlier, is concerned primarily with the behaviour of the economy and its implications; the banking economist's work is directed principally towards monetary and banking trends; that of the corporate finance economist deals with the capital structure while the investment economists, who can be divided between industrial and monetary specialists, deal with industrial and monetary trends respectively and the bearing they have on investment.

Needless to say demarcation lines among these areas in each of which considerable advance has been and continues to be made, are not as yet clear-cut and the fields overlap in some cases to quite a considerable extent. Where the economic department is small, its members must cover a large number of fields; in larger departments there is much greater degree of specialisation.

Of the four special fields mentioned, banking specialists are mostly found in the banks; general economists are common to all institutions providing the broad framework within which business can operate, while investment economists are attached to broking offices, insurance companies and merchant banks. Corporate finance economists are at present mainly confined to merchant banks.

While the requirements expected from City economists are exacting the career prospects are exciting and promising. As described above economists in the City perform essentially a staff function closely related to policy making and co-ordination, but they also have opportunities of moving to the executive side of business and general management. This has been quite common in the City, where a number of economists have moved to management posts with outstanding success. Indeed, it can be said that experience in the economic department is extremely valuable as a training ground for future managers and directors.

Both the financial and status prospects of economists in the City compare very favourably with other professions. The young graduate joining the economic department is looked upon as

K

a specialist and rewarded accordingly. His initial salary is likely to be within the range of £1,000–£1,250. By his late twenties for the average man it should be around £2,000 and for those at the top of the profession above £2,500. The median salary of those in the second half of the thirties tends to lie near £3,500 with prospects of good progression later on. For the above average man the salary path is even better. The status ladder of the economists in the City is also attractive. In many economic departments they progress toward full managerial status, the heads of such departments often assume the position of a fully fledged economic adviser with prospects of a seat on the Board. This is also true of other institutions, while partnerships in brokers' offices can be obtained fairly early in the cycle of one's working life.

The broad pattern of functional responsibilities and the career path now emerging in the City is likely to become even more pronounced in the future. Economists by their training have always been concerned with policy matters and their consequences. With the growth of professionalism and their own skills they can provide a valuable contribution to the working of financial institutions and of the City at large. That their services were needed and appreciated is shown by the growing demand for them. The contribution which they make to the efficiency of the City needs no other testimonial.

9

The Economist in the Investment Business

by P. J. Cropper

The investment business has three main functions, security dealing, portfolio management, and the reorganisation of capital in connection with new issues, acquisitions etc. It is organised into a large number of independent units, most of which are small in terms of personnel. Consequently those problems of internal organisation, finance, and trading policy, with which the business economist is often concerned in large scale industry, do not arise in the typical unit of the investment business. Furthermore very few economists are employed in the City specifically as economists, that is as full time analysts of general trends in economic, industrial and monetary affairs. On the other hand everybody concerned with policy must know something of the subject because economic judgements enter into most investment decisions. Thus most economists who enter the investment world soon find themselves either involved in the day to day business of banking, broking or portfolio management, or find themselves specialising on an investment analysis. If they pursue the latter course they will become members of a stimulating new profession in which economists, accountants and actuaries are struggling to evolve techniques suited to the measurement of business efficiency and of the true return on capital.

Main Forms of Organisation

There are five main forms of business organisation involved in investment:

(i) *Joint Stock Banks*

The 'Big Five'—Barclays, Lloyds, Midland, National Provincial and Westminster are large organisations each employing upwards of twenty thousand personnel, the great bulk of whom are concerned with the clearing functions of the bank and with the numerous services provided through branch offices. Apart from the highly specialised work of investing their own assets in Government securities the banks are mainly involved in investment work on an advisory basis. Their Trustee Departments are responsible for large sums of money invested in stocks and shares but neither they nor the branch offices carrying out day to day investment work for customers normally decide policy without reference to stockbroking firms, which are consulted as experts. The recent launching of unit trusts by some of the Big Five may, however, be indicative of a more positive involvement by the banks in investment management.

The banks have central economic sections which provide general service to the departments and branches and are usually involved in preparing the Bank Reviews. These sections naturally employ trained economists but otherwise a new entrant to a Joint Stock Bank will be best advised to forget his specialisation just as he would on entering the administrative grade of the Civil Service, and submit himself to the bank's normal training routine.

(ii) *Insurance Companies*

As in branch banking, only a small minority of insurance staffs are employed on investment work. But the insurance companies are a major force in the investment world; the fact that most of their funds are continually growing gives them a particularly powerful influence in the market, where they are the archetypal 'institutions', setting the tone of business by their day to day policies. Their shareholdings give the insurance companies powerful voting power in most public companies, but up till now this has seldom been openly used. The specialist *élite* in insurance are the actuaries; their training centres on the calculation of mortality, accident and similar risks, but it includes advanced work on investment, and actuaries are often employed in the investment departments. There is occasional recruitment from outside straight into these departments, but otherwise there is little direct employment of economists except in the one or two large insurance companies which have specialist economic departments.

(iii) *Merchant Banks*

Whereas the basis of Joint Stock Banking is the branch business, most of the merchant banks operate from their London offices, with few branches, and concern themselves more with permanent industrial finance and with international business. They pride themselves on the diversity of services offered to their commercial customers and this usually covers most aspects of capital reorganisation and of portfolio management. Merchant banking is a highly personal form of business and the banks bear very closely the imprint of their directors' personalities. Most business is done at a high level in clients' firms, so that personal connections and contacts are vital to success; there has lately been a tendency for the merchant banks to recruit men who have already attained eminence in the law, accountancy and the Civil Service.

(iv) *Portfolio and Investment Management*

The management of investment trusts and unit trusts is often undertaken by merchant banks, although there are also several independent trust management firms. In Scotland particularly, trust management is a speciality of accountants and lawyers. The needs of smaller portfolios are met by firms of Investment Consultants, who bring professional skill to an area where small scale operation and remoteness from the market have become an increasing disadvantage. Openings in these smaller management organisations tend to be filled by men with experience gained in one of the larger offices such as those of a stockbroker or an insurance company.

Finally many of the larger commercial and industrial firms now run their own pension funds with the aid of consulting actuaries. The investment work sometimes falls within the company secretary's province but more often it requires a separate department. These funds are growing very fast as employers' and members' contributions build up and their exemption from income tax and capital gains tax puts them in an exceptionally favourable position. Although pension funds in the United Kingdom do not normally buy substantial share-holdings in their own companies, they do between them now hold an influential holding in most quoted companies and it will be interesting to see how they use their power in the next ten years.

(v) *Stock Exchange Firms*

Stockbrokers handle the bulk of security transactions in the United Kingdom. Their minimum commission rates are fixed by the Council of the Stock Exchange, so that competition takes the form of services, which are usually provided free as an adjunct to the basic dealing function. These services include portfolio valuations and reviews for smaller clients and the provision of investment reports and studies to the institutions. Stockbroking firms also engage in company work and capital reconstruction, where they sometimes act in conjunction with the merchant banks and sometimes in competition with them.

The post war years have been a boom time for stockbroking, although jobbing has become progressively less profitable, due to institutional factors and a changing pattern of business. During the 1950's and early 1960's there were many openings for graduates in brokers' offices, partly a reflection of the low recruitment level during the hard years between 1930 and 1950. Since 1962 the trend of prosperity has levelled out, but rapid changes in technique give scope for versatile minds.

A large broking firm is a complex organisation. It will probably have between a dozen and twenty partners (the legal limit of twenty partners has been removed by the new Companies Act), a staff of up to three hundred, and five principal departments:

(i) a dealing staff responsible for carrying out the actual business of buying and selling on the floor of the Stock Exchange,

(ii) a portfolio management and advisory department dealing with the affairs of private clients, of trustees and of bank investment departments,

(iii) a research department carrying out investment analysis and preparing special reports.

(iv) an institutional department, providing an advisory and dealing department for the use of insurance companies, investment trusts and other large funds,

(v) behind the scenes a substantial general office, handling the detailed work of accounting and of settlement with clients, jobbers, banks and other brokers. This is at present an area of intense experimental interest to the computer companies.

An economic training can be useful in all these departments, in providing a key to understanding what goes on. But it can at most be only one qualification for success. For example, the dealing staff on the floor of the House need to know little about the actual companies whose stock they are handling; for them the most important thing is to earn a reputation for straight dealing and to observe the customs which have been devised to soften the competitive edge of relationships in a community where bargaining takes place year in and year out at very close quarters. In dealing with private portfolios, again the job is often seen to lie not so much in managing clients' portfolios for them as in providing a sympathetic professional service of advice akin to that provided by the family solicitor. Brokers do not normally undertake the responsibility of management; their function is to advise and there is a natural tendency towards caution.

On the institutional side, by contrast, the emphasis is on salesmanship. A broker earns commission by persuading investment managers to deal with him, rather than with someone else. This may be accomplished in many different ways. It can be done by offering him tempting propositions and lines of stock or by providing an efficient service of industrial or market information; it can be done by making share recommendations that have a knack of turning out well, or it may be done by striking up a basis of mutual liking and respect on the golf course which then spreads through to an efficient but not particularly intellectual dealing arrangement. The relationship between a successful broker and his institutional client is a subtle blend; all-round alertness is often more useful than strong views, great knowledge or profound economic thinking.

The complexity of the stockbroking business renders it a difficult one to organise. This, together with problems inherent in the financial structure of partnership, can often result in instability, with personal relationships frequently under strain. A smooth running business makes a good deal of money when business is brisk but when activity falls off the partners are reminded that their personal liability is unlimited. The financing problem can in practice detract considerably from the attractions of the career. With personality and ability it has not been difficult in the past few years to attain membership of the Stock Exchange and often the status of partnership in a firm. Recently, however, capital requirements for Stock Exchange firms have been raised very sharply following a number of spectacular defaults. An average sum of around £10,000 per partner is now needed by broking firms—and the ambitious young graduate who does not have the expectation of this sort of wealth must face a longish period in which his partnership is more apparent than real. For the research man the limitations are more severe again, as he will often find that the tone of the partnership is set by the salesmen who bring in the hard cash rather than by the analyst who does the backroom work. But despite the background of instability—or maybe because of it—stockbroking offers scope for responsibility and independent judgement at an earlier age than most other forms of business.

The Management and Analysis of Investments

With the capital at his disposal an investment manager needs to set out with certain well defined objectives. In a sense his object is always the same—to maximise the total return on his capital with the minimum possible risk. But that definition verges on the truistic. More detail is needed. For example, the manager must have a clear idea how far he is investing in order to obtain the income needed to meet fixed commitments, or whether he can hazard the capital in riskier investments for the chance of a greater ultimate return. He needs to know whether income is needed immediately or whether he should concentrate primarily on building up the capital value of his fund in order to establish greater income flows in future. He needs to have a

view on future exchange rates of the countries in whose
securities he is investing, and he must bear in mind the position
of his fund *vis à vis* the different forms of taxation to which it is
exposed.

The management problem is then to pick that selection of
securities which will most nearly result in fulfilment of the
objectives of the fund. The existence of uncertainty rules out the
logical extreme of selecting one 'best buy' and investing the
whole fund in it: risk spreading is enforced by the fact that the
most assured forecast of the behaviour of a single security
can be brought to nothing by an unforeseen change of circumstances. Since there are over nine thousand quoted securities in
the U.K. alone, some system of selection must be developed.

At this point the analytical process begins. Securities must be
grouped and classified according to their various characteristics.
Their riskiness must be assessed in relation to the degree of risk
permitted in the portfolio, current returns must be calculated
and, where possible, future returns estimated. Only when he
knows his market inside out can the investment manager feel
ready to start choosing his portfolio—and only if he remains
constantly abreast of changing patterns in these markets can he
ensure that the portfolio is adjusted to meet external circumstances.

It is possible to identify four main groups of investment:

(i) The fixed interest securities of governments and of official
bodies backed by government guarantees.

(ii) The quoted securities of private enterprise companies.

(iii) Unquoted shares in private companies.

(iv) Property and real estate.

The significance of a Stock Exchange quotation which dis-
tinguishes (ii) from (iii) above is one of marketability. It is in
most circumstances possible to dispose of an interest in a quoted
company; but a holder of shares in an unquoted company is
locked in unless he can find an interested buyer and negotiate a
sale directly to him. This situation often results in the investor
having to become involved in management in order to protect
his money, and goes beyond what is normally meant by portfolio investment. Investment in property is also a special subject
requiring specific qualifications.

The process of assessment involves two techniques—calculation and analysis. The more imprecise the data, the more the mathematician has to yield to the analyst, whose experience lies in making estimates where there are no hard facts. Mathematical techniques are primarily applicable to the fixed interest securities issued by governments and quasi-governmental bodies. On the basis of information about the interest to be paid on a bond, its life and its repayment terms, it is possible to calculate the yields obtainable by a holder. Even then it is not possible for the investor to make a final judgement on the relative merits of different bonds without considering monetary influences and interest rates. For example, it is foolish to buy today a security with a life of twenty years if one believes that, because of the immediate trend of monetary affairs, it may be possible to buy the same stock at a lower price six weeks hence. Similarly, the differential movements of long and short term interest rates need to be considered in making the decision whether to hold long or short dated bonds.

Mathematical techniques are rather less adequate on their own when it comes to the fixed interest obligations of private enterprise organisations i.e. debentures and preference shares. Although the same yield calculations can be made, figures alone may not tell the investor which of a bunch of companies is in actual danger of going bankrupt—the main circumstance when a fixed interest security can turn out to be a really unsound holding.

When it comes to ordinary shares, the mathematician is able to contribute little, and the field is wide open to the investment analyst, relying on all the normal arts of business assessment. These arts are fundamentally those of an applied economist.

Techniques of Equity Analysis

Techniques of ordinary share analysis have only taken root in the United Kingdom since the war. It was not until 1948 that the Companies Act enforced the publication of consolidated accounts for companies, including their subsidiaries, and it was several years later before a worthwhile body of comparative information had been built up. Even now in 1967 many companies are only beginning to publish their turnover figures, which are invaluable in any calculation of profitability. But the combined efforts of the Stock Exchange, the press, and analysts themselves have done much to break down the traditional secrecy in which companies formerly veiled their affairs even from their own shareholders.

At present most offices have their own approach to analysis of ordinary shares, and the arrival of computers has brought the ferment of interest to an exceptionally high pitch. This is not the place to enter into a thorough survey, but broadly speaking the following steps are common ground:

(i) Examination of the company's past performance expressed in terms of turnover, profits and dividends, return of capital and per share earnings.

(ii) Assessment of the company's position in the economy and its likely future progress as a trading entity, and hence of its future performance in terms of earnings and dividends.

(iii) Judgement of the likely effect of these future developments on the movement of the share price.

This process leads towards an estimate of the return expected from a particular security over a given period, made up of dividend and capital growth, and an expression of the risk or uncertainty involved. There is, of course, a natural tendency for high risk to go with high predicted return, and low risk is usually co-ordinated with low return. Much of the art in investment consists of spotting anomalies in this correlation—shares which at their ruling market price offer an above average combination of prospective return and freedom from risk.

The Price Element

The investment man is generally working at one remove from business, through the medium of shares bought on the Stock Exchange. This introduces two factors which are not normally involved in direct entrepreneurship or in market research work, namely management and share price.

Management as a factor of production fits logically into the economist's view of things and the assessment of it can be at once a fascinating and tantalising job. It may be quite apparent to an investment analyst that a particular company is in the right country and the right industry at the right time; but if the management muffs the play then all is to no avail. Similarly, some enterprises now ranking among the top hundred have been ranked as outsiders in their early days because of doubts about their management, doubts which have later turned out to be unmerited. Evaluation of all this is something which can only come with experience. The same is true of company financing which is another important element in the making of a successful business. The decision whether to finance expansion internally, to borrow on fixed interest securities, or to raise money by an ordinary share issue—or not to expand at all—is one which vitally affects the value of the existing shares in a company. Many take-over battles have been won by bidders who have known how to exploit weaknesses in the financial management of their victims.

Analysts are divided on the value of direct contact with management. Some will say that an outsider visiting a company is vulnerable to false impressions and that management is best judged by its past record of achievement. But this method fails when it comes to prompt detection of a change in the quality or morale of a company's senior staff. By the time the figures are out the damage has been done. There is still a lot of truth in the old saying 'It's not what you know, but who you know'—not necessarily in the sense that close friends will reveal business confidences, but because knowledge about the hopes and aspirations of management can provide a valuable clue to future trends.

Price is the ultimate arbiter of the analyst's world. It is not sufficient for him to reach a well argued conclusion about the future progress of an enterprise; he must also make a judgement about the impact of these developments, if they occur, on the price of the company's shares, It is essential. furthermore, to distinguish between the concepts of value and price. In a free and volatile market such as exists in most securities the influence of something akin to fashion often produces a wide discrepancy between the price of a share and what analysts would suspect to be its intrinsic value. Prices tend to move together, influenced by the state of the economy and of the capital market in which they exist, in disregard of the particular circumstances of individual companies.

There are few analysts today who would go all the way with the extreme protagonists of technical analysis, regarding price as a result entirely of disembodied supply and demand forces and professing to select their investments simply on the basis of price trends plotted on charts. Equally, nobody would attempt to assess a share simply by calculating the underlying value of the assets and goodwill it represents. The truth is many sided. The one fact that has to be learnt in investment is that to buy shares in a company with demonstrably good prospects is not a sure way to make money. In the first place, others may have recognised the situation already, and by their buying forced up the price so that it already discounts the expected benefits. Secondly the influence of extraneous occurrences, such as adverse trends in the economy as a whole, may serve to nullify the gains foreseen for this individual share price through a general depression of markets.

Conclusion

Keynes had some scathing things to say in the 'General Theory' about the efficiency of stock markets in allocating capital. Since the middle 1930's when he was writing there have been great improvements brought about largely by better information and by the responsible approach of large institutions concerned with investing other people's money. Yet it is hard to feel that the practice of investment will ever reach the point where it could be called a science. Meanwhile the economist will find in it a continuously fascinating and continuously changing kaleidoscope of problems which will utilise most of what he has learnt in the theoretical and practical training of his subject.

10

The Economist in the Public Service

by RALPH TURVEY

An engineer or an architect in the public service is either directly exercising his professional skill on a particular task for which he is responsible or, when he is more senior, exercising it indirectly in supervising junior professional staff. He may spend some of his time sitting on committees and looking after administrative chores, but by and large he is an expert engaged in doing a job which no one else can do. If he is promoted far enough this will no longer be true, but in that case he is no longer employed as an engineer or architect; he is an administrator who got to the top via a particular profession.

The role of the economist in the public service is rather different. He is much more rarely regarded as someone whose expertise automatically makes him the appropriate person for a particular task and who is left with sole responsibility for it. There are two reasons for this, one good and one bad. The bad one is that nearly everyone likes to be his own economist. People are thus readier to accept the professional expertise of, say, the engineer—who deals with a field where they are aware of their own ignorance—than they are to accept the views of the economist. They usually have their own view on economic matters; indeed most people have some rough explicit and inconsistent analytical structure at the back of their minds which they are ready to apply to any economic problem.

The good reason for not giving economists any executive responsibility is of course partly that they do not really know very much about the working of the economy and partly that economic problems involve political questions. No one, I think, would attach as much weight to an economist's prediction (e.g. of the fall in the price level that would be produced by the abolition of some specified import duties) as to an engineer's (e.g. whether a given load would cause a bridge to collapse). Thus even if no politics were involved, it is not entirely silly to say that economic policy is too important to leave to economists.

These attitudes of administrators and politicians to economics are reflected in the role given to economists in the public service. There are only three areas where the possession of some special expertise by economists is regarded as justifying the delegation to them of some autonomy. One is forecasting, another is background economic research and a third, which may be developing into an accepted area of professional competence, is cost-benefit analysis.

Take forecasting first. Economists are employed to make forecasts more than for anything else and they are given a freer hand in forecasting than in any other sphere. This seems to me to be true not only of Whitehall and the nationalised industries but also of private industry, commerce and finance. It is explained by the average man's (correct) belief that he cannot foresee the future; the relatively few people who think they can are mainly addicts of curve-fitting.

Now this popular esteem of economists as forecasters is rather unfortunate. Economists are not particularly good at judging the relative likelihood of each of a specified set of future possible outcomes. What they can do well is merely to organise thought systematically so that the guessing required to make a forecast is clearly specified by isolating an appropriate number of causally relevant factors. Asked to predict X, the economist systematically lists the determinants of X and describes their relationship to X. He can do this better than a non-economist because he knows more about the way the economy works. He has, that is to say, a coherent and well-organised analysis of what has determined X in the past and he may even be able to quantify some of the relationships. But this is knowledge about the past, not clairvoyance.

Thus while economists do have a comparative advantage in forecasting, it is an advantage in method rather than in the use of any given method. Since forecasting is so crucial for fiscal policy and for the investment programmes of the nationalised industries it seems to be too important for Ministers and the

Boards of nationalised industries to delegate. This suggests, therefore, that the economists' role would be to present a sort of menu of key assumptions about the future from which the decision-makers would choose. Once their choice was made, the final working out of a forecast would be mere arithmetic; the hard work and the expertise on the part of the economist would lie in the background analysis designed to pick out and quantify the influence of the key assumptions which are presented to the decision-makers for choice. We might call this parametric forecasting.

There is much less to be said about the general acceptance of the idea that economic research can be left to economists to do on their own. The difficulty in practice is that once the researcher gets to know something about a particular subject his advice and co-operation in practical policy making become valuable. If the administrators recognise this, they may leave him inadequate time to complete his research. Thus we have the paradox that it is not always desirable for the economist's advice to be highly valued by his colleagues.

It may be argued that this merely means that research ought to be done in academic institutions and that the problem only arises if the researcher is wrongly located inside the public sector. But this is to disregard the countervailing point that close contact is often necessary if research is to be fruitful; thus an outsider may be too unaware of the facts of life or of the availability of information in a nationalised industry to be able to work usefully on some of its problems. I frequently feel that the aspects of electricity supply which interest academic economists are non-problems.

A readiness to let economists be in charge of cost-benefit analyses which leads to the making of decisions has not yet been shown in this country. It may come, however, if the fashionability of the idea and the current respect for Rand-type contributions to U.S. defence policy continue to be in tune with the times. Recent experience in transport, fuel and overseas aid suggest that Ministerial sympathy for the application of economics to policy can produce pretty rapid change in the role of economists in Whitehall.

But this lies in the future. Leaving forecasting and research

L

on one side, what else do economists in the public service do? The answer is simply that they sit on committees and they write minutes. These may be called something different such as Working Groups and Memoranda but, however they are named, the job consists essentially of communicating with non-economists by talking and writing. It is less presumptuous than it sounds to say that all this basically boils down to educating the non-economist by one means or another, but it is just as true as the complementary proposition that the non-economists educate the economist. The point is that policy recommendations are formulated by a dialogue between the representatives of different parts of the organisation and various kinds of expert. This is as true of a Whitehall Working Party on, say, the control of office building in the south-east as it is of a Panel set up by the electricity industry to formulate recommendations on industrial tariff policy. The process of education is mutual and it is (usually) constructive. I do not mean by this that committees always advance the state of knowledge and produce useful recommendations. They do not. I merely mean that the economist emerges with a better understanding of the problem than he had to start with and that, if he has done his job properly, the same will be true of the non-economist members of the group.

Before going on to discuss the limited but important kind of education which the economist gives to his non-economist colleagues, it is worth considering what sort of education he picks up in return. A more lively sense of what is practical than is possessed by most academic economists is one kind of gain. Another is the discovery that nearly everything is more complicated than it looks to the outsider. Third, one picks up a superficial acquaintance with the technology of the industry or problem involved. These benefits all sound trite and it is difficult to explain how real and important they are. They can be acquired by experience but not by formal education.

There is some danger that the economist in the public service may learn these lessons too well and lose some of his special usefulness. Excessive awareness of the multiple facets of reality destroys the cutting edge of analysis by inhibiting the abstraction of a few key features from that reality for rigorous treatment. If the economist becomes unwilling to simplify in this way by disregarding many facets, he becomes unable to apply a clearly articulated structure of thought to his problem, he ceases to be a scientist with a specific kind of contribution to make and becomes no different from the administrators with whom he works. The economist, qua economist, should leave many avenues unexplored and many stones unturned; let others do the job of synthesis, his task is not to be a wise old man but to put forward one type of view and one kind of analysis for general consideration.

A related danger is that economists in the public service may be so busy inter-acting with non-economists that they have insufficient time for keeping up with other economists. Ten years out of touch with the professional literature and an economist begins to become obsolete. Since he will be ten years' wiser in terms of other knowledge and experience, he will of course be much more useful than when he started the job, so that neither he nor his colleagues may notice his obsolescence. All that I am saying is that nine and a half years' experience plus six months' reading would be better still.

How much economists manage to keep up to date with that fraction of the subject which is relevant to their work seems to depend partly upon their personalities and not only upon their employer's attitude. Those of them who regard reading the occasional paper in one of the journals as an essential part of their work seem to be those who do such reading, while one suspects that those who plead lack of time sometimes also suffer a lack of interest. This latter group still deal with economic problems and still learn more and more as time passes, but they become less professional as economists and more professional as administrators. This is fine—why should economists not have the same chance of rising in the administrative hierarchy as anyone else? There is a potential danger in it only if the professional obsolescence goes unrecognised; the wise man will seek the reinforcement of younger professional economists so that, as one such eminent man put it, he was 'in a position to ignore the best advice'.

I do not for an instant wish to suggest that the tremendous amount of economic research which is done outside the public service is all of a sort which economists there can ignore only at their peril. In fact a very large fraction of academic economics seems to be for ostentation rather than for use. But if many writings on demand theory are mere *jeux d'esprit*, there has been some admirable empirically-orientated work on the demand for durable goods. Attempts to estimate oversimplified production functions by econometric analysis of inferior data in cases where the engineers already know whether or not there are constant returns to scale put the profession in disrepute, but some of the work on inventory policy makes up for that. Some ignorance about the consumption function has been dissipated. These are just a few casual examples of recent research but they do show that there are some matters where keeping up to date is important in relation to real problems which are currently relevant in Whitehall or the nationalised industries.

Turning now to what the economist contributes, outside those preserves of forecasting, background research and (potentially) cost benefit analysis which may be put in charge of economists, generalisation is difficult. The economist is there to contribute an apparatus of thought and some institutional knowledge. Just what he contributes must depend on the economic sophistication of his non-economist colleagues which can vary enormously. At an elementary level the economist may, for example, have to spend much time and effort at meetings or on paper explaining

(a) the nature of input-output analysis;
(b) the relevance of marginal rather than average quantities in maximisation problems;
(c) the irrelevance of depreciation as measured by accountants to (the non-tax aspects of) investment decisions;
(d) consumers' surplus versus revenue as measures of the benefits from an indivisible investment.

This is all textbook stuff, though the textbooks rarely put it in the way needed for a committee. University teachers spend three years teaching students such matters and even then do not expect the fresh graduate to be automatically aware when and how they are relevant in a policy context. So the task of getting such principles across within a few minutes or a few pages is not an easy one. Indeed, passing from university teaching to economic advising involves giving up the easy task of setting essays to undergraduates for the more difficult one of having them set by

Under-Secretaries! Explaining the welfare economics arguments for marginal cost pricing to a group of officials is quite a problem when their desire to abandon the subject grows exponentially with time, when one of them is a fervent postaliser and the chairman is a firm (but subconscious) adherent of the labour theory of value.

Keynes once said that everyone is the slave of some defunct economist. (He really meant that a popularised and incorrect version of some writers' thoughts eventually becomes popular currency. Thus, as I said earlier, every man likes to be his own economist.) Faced at times with the impossibly demanding task of getting across a large fraction of the corpus of economic analysis in the space of a few minutes the economist may sometimes feel it realistic to limit his ambitions, merely hoping to become such a defunct economist!

Having spoken of the extreme case, it is proper to pass to the opposite extreme. Both in Whitehall and in the nationalised industries there are some non-economists who are such only formally. In my personal experience this has been strikingly the case with those electrical engineers who have specialised in system planning. The sophistication of their approach to optimising investment in generating plant is such that economists could learn a great deal by studying it. This, incidentally, holds as much for the U.S. and Britain, where economists have played no role in system planning, as in France where they have.

The simple fact is that people who are concerned with the application of quantitative techniques to optimisation problems have a lot in common, whatever their basic disciplines. The engineer and the economist who both know something of linear programming can each formulate their ideas in terms which are comprehensible to the other. Communication is thus easy where the problem is to maximise something. It is much more difficult in analysing the functioning of the economy, where the economist does know a little more than the non-economist about the economic behaviour of people and institutions. An engineer who is crystal-clear on replacement investment criteria may easily commit the fallacy of composition when talking about fiscal policy. The special knowledge of the economist may not amount to very much, but even the ability to avoid error is an important attribute in a field where muddle and ignorance reign.

Perhaps the most important contributions which the economist in public service can make are, first, a propensity to take an economy-wide view and, second, a sense of the ability (and limitations) of the price mechanism to allocate resources. The first of these is important even in Whitehall, where the narrowness of departmental interests can sometimes be pronounced. A trivial example which illustrates this well is the unwillingness of a generally research-minded civil servant to show any interest in a proposed piece of research relating to a problem which concerned two other departments beside his own. The economist's notion of the public interest may be very narrow but it is at least intellectually coherent and thus can serve to anchor a discussion. The lay administrator, more vaguely aware of a larger number of considerations, may be unable to focus his discussion in national terms and instead will then fall back on a series of *ad hoc desiderata* which are the particular concern of his department. The Home Office has never bothered much about the effects of shop hours legislation upon competition in retailing and the reform of local government finance has not interested the Treasury, even though considerations of both equity and fiscal efficiency suggest that national and local taxation deserve joint examination. The feeling for interdependence inculcated by a study of general equilibrium theory is thus of some importance.

The economist in the nationalised industries has less to contribute as an antidote to parochialism because of the role of the market in regulating the activities of these industries. The salutory competition between the electricity and gas industries, for instance, replaces abstract questions of fuel policy by concrete questions of gaining or losing consumers so far as the commercial departments are concerned.

The economist, aware of the economic aspects of the public interest and, with perfect logic, insisting that consistent choice necessarily involves the maximisation or minimisation of something, is inclined to ask what is the objective function which decision-makers are trying to maximise or minimise. He learns that, as suggested above, few non-economists have what he can accept as an adequate economic concept of the public interest. This is why I have suggested that the economist has an important role here, despite the limitations of his own horizons. Thus its happens that when people need criteria for making (or justifying) their decisions and when they lack coherent ones on economic matters, they will invent others. The classic example of this is the use of the words 'fair and reasonable' to describe cost allocations which purport to answer questions of fact. More generally, decisions are regarded as fair or unfair in terms solely of their impact upon inanimate bodies corporate. Thus the economist may be surprised to find that he is the one who has to point out that the consideration of fairness which ought to be brought in to the argument relates to real people.

All this may suggest that economists do or should give advice which is essentially political. Those who think in terms of means-end dichotomies may find this shocking. Now it is impossibly difficult to define and preserve in practice the sort of abstention from value-judgements that Lord Robbins wrote about over thirty years ago. But that sort of abstention is different from political neutrality as practised by the Civil Service, and which can be practised just as well by economists as by any other civil servants. The philosophical discussion missed the practical point that a politician can smell an antipathetic value-judgement a mile away and wants his advisers to work on the basis of the value-judgements he does hold. So an economist in Whitehall will submit a scheme for an export incentive equally readily to a Conservative or Labour government, but will not bother a Labour Chancellor with plans for abolishing surtax or a Conservative Minister with proposals for nationalisation. In other words, one does not waste everyone's time by putting up suggestions which are not going to be acceptable. If one doesn't know what is acceptable, one can learn by experience. Thus there are only two rules, one of prudence: do not gain a reputation for proposing what is unacceptable; and one of intellectual honesty: do not conceal value-judgements. But that is all, and in the context of political decisions the economist cannot escape value-judgements.

Since 1964, a few economists have gone to Whitehall who would scarcely regard themselves as politically neutral. So long as this does not threaten the independence of those who are, it seems to be an entirely welcome development. Such a threat would arise if political and non-political posts were not clearly distinguished, since in this case the non-political successor to a political predecessor might be unwarrantably labelled as political. This could either prevent his taking the job or impede his performance if he did take it.

The second of the two particular contributions of the economist mentioned above was his understanding of the potentialities of the price mechanism. This contribution was exemplified in the last war by the introduction of points rationing, and a current manifestation of it is the interest being shown in road pricing. This may seem just an intellectual plaything, but so did the use of parking-meters as anything but a time-rationing device ten years ago. Nowadays, the idea that geographical differentials in meter charges should be related to geographical differences in the scarcity of parking space is much more acceptable. Twenty years ago, marginal cost pricing policy in public enterprises formed the subject of lively theoretical discussion in the learned journals. Nowadays, Whitehall is interested in these ideas. This would not have happened but for the economists employed there. Another field of economic policy where an understanding of the price mechanism, albeit limited in empirical terms, gives economists the ability to think constructively is the balance of payments. Non-economists fail to consider a floating rate as seriously as it deserves.

On a sophisticated theoretical level, economists have become a little more careful in describing the ability of a price mechanism to co-ordinate the economic decisions of independent entities than were such classic writings as those of Lerner and Lange. Since forward markets are not omnipresent, the co-ordination of forward plans is not achieved by the price mechanism. This is one rationalisation of the need for a national economic plan, whether this is viewed as co-ordinated commitments to action (at one extreme) or just as socialised market research (at the other). But whatever one thinks of the Plan we have got, there can be no doubt that it owes its statistical coherence to the economists and statisticians of the D.E.A. This brings us back, finally, from the general approach of economists to their special expertise. The knowledge of social accounting, macro-economics and so on which was required to put the Plan together with reasonable consistency is technical knowledge. There are some distinguished non-economist civil servants who have imbibed a lot of this knowledge, but they have imbibed it from their economist colleagues. So here is an example of something which economists contribute over and above simple awareness that demand curves slope downwards, bygones are bygones and so on. As knowledge advances the range of such things will expand. It sounds, then, as though the scope for economists in public service will continue to increase even though general understanding of economic matters is far greater than it used to be.

11

The Work of an Economic Consultant

by W. F. LUTTRELL

Definition

The recent growth in 'economic consultancy' has led to the term being used to cover an extraordinarily wide range of activities. Firms using this title on the Continent, for example, sometimes embrace within it practice in industrial psychology, marketing and advertising advice, operational research, financial advice, staff recruitment, and almost the whole range of management consultancy as regards the internal operation of the firm, as well as industrial market research and the impact of sectoral changes in the economy on a field in which a firm is interested. But a much narrower definition will be used here, since the writer will be describing his own experience. Briefly, it is the study of the external situation that the client firm is and will be facing—both as regards the economy in general and the particular sectors it is interested in—together with the implications and opportunities that this will provide for the client, bearing in mind its organisation and resources.

Consultancy Organisation

We are discussing here a medium-sized consultancy with a staff of around forty, over half of whom are graduate economists with industrial experience. Part-time and temporary staff are seldom used, but other specialist agencies are brought in when appropriate; and where a study includes a survey of householders or other very large samples, this part of the work is sub-contracted to a consumer sample survey firm with a national interviewing force. The office organisation is kept as simple as possible, with a minimum of administration; and office jobs like stencil-typing and duplicating, photo-printing, collating and binding of reports, as well as computer runs, are given out to specialist firms available nearby, which generally do them efficiently and quickly. A simple costing system operates for the consultancy's own jobs, with monthly balances, and a quarterly overall profit-and-loss account.

Fields of Work

Most of the consultancy's work involves some industrial market research and field surveys, but the purpose is usually to assist the client firm in its marketing or development strategy. (Work is also done in the public sector, on the economics of urban growth, regional studies, and the development of industrial complexes, but it is not discussed here.)

The kind of situation that often induces a firm to call in a consultant is when it is considering a major investment for expansion. It may have reached capacity in an existing plant and be considering whether to build a completely new one, perhaps with much greater capacity, incorporating the latest manufacturing techniques, which may also involve changes in economies of scale. In such a case, assessments of the present and future size of market, and of the conditions under which it could attain a given market share, would be the information it would seek: these when taken with capital and operating cost assessments, would provide the basis for estimates of profitability and return on capital.

Another example would be when a firm wished to re-examine its marketing strategy for a product or service, especially where the nature of the market (and the behaviour of its competitors) was changing and was expected to change further. This might also involve the possibility of mergers, acquisitions, or further specialisation.

Again, the firm may be thinking of extending its market, either geographically or by widening its range to related activities, and want to know in detail what conditions it would face.

A final example, and perhaps the most awkward for the consultant, is the firm in a declining market that wishes to 'diversify': its executives are apt to feel a strong attraction towards glamorous or highly technical activities where someone else is making a good profit but where innocents are quickly slaughtered.

As regards the size of the client firm, nearly all the work comes from large or very large companies, often ones that are equipped to carry out some studies for themselves but like to put out major jobs, especially those that involve fieldwork as well as overall assessment. Others may have had a different experience, but this writer has found that while occasional jobs are done for firms with net assets of £1 million or so, the great majority of work is from firms of £10 million and upwards. There seem to be several reasons. The large firms have more room for manoeuvre, in that they can re-allocate resources. If they have a large share of the market, or would need such a share to operate successfully, changes in the external situation and in the market growth-rate will be more important to them: the small firm with less than one per cent of the market will be less concerned with these aspects though it will of course mind about price competition, but it may have found a relatively sheltered corner of the market. Lastly there is the question of cost: a small firm may have quite a wide range of products or activities, and a study for it may cost nearly as much for a firm with ten times the turnover in the same field. Successful studies for small firms have mostly concerned those with a narrow range of specialist activities and a single well-defined new development in mind.

As to the fields of product or service, the majority of clients are manufacturers, with a preponderance in industrial products and secondly in consumer durables, and with some in food products. But the field is very wide. A lot of work has been concerned with the building and construction industry; a good deal has been for wholesalers, though less for retailers; several studies have been in catering and related services; and a growing amount is in the transport industry. But again, this experience may not be typical.

The future time-scale to which the studies refer is usually of the order of five years, with a broader assessment for say ten years ahead. This follows from the main purpose, which is usually for marketing or development strategy in the longer run, rather than for short term forecasting of the next few months; but clearly the cyclical position in the next year or so must often be brought into account. Occasionally one's best guess of trends for much longer periods ahead is also required: for example, in the case of plant with a longer life, or where a licensing and royalty agreement for say twenty years is involved.

Client-Consultancy Relations

It has been mentioned that the economic consultant's purpose is generally to study the external situation that the client will be facing, and to assess the implications for the client's future course of action. To do this effectively, he must not only study the operation of the market or field of action concerned, and the economic environment, but must also have a good understanding of the client's own organisation, its facilities, personnel and methods of operation. Without this, he would not know to what extent the success of future strategies might be affected by the constraints and latent opportunities inherent in the firm, both in a physical sense and as regards skills and attitudes. Naturally, the depth of knowledge needed will depend on the tasks, but the point to be made is that even a primarily 'external' study should be related to internal conditions to achieve the best results, and this applies to the devising of the study as much as to its use after completion.

However, a new client will often regard the commissioning of a study as a matter simply of defining the market they want to have examined: the consultant, after agreeing a fee and completion date, will go away and return in a few months' time with a handsome report. This may look impressive, but quite apart from the fact that there will be no interpretation for its application to the company's problems and possible strategies, there may well have been a misallocation of resources in the carrying out of the study. Even an apparently straightforward 'market' or sector of the economy is usually quite complex when examined in detail, and knowledge of it is never complete, particularly as regards the ways in which it may change in future. The essential thing is to devise the study so that it will give the maximum help to the client in his future policy decisions, and therefore to concentrate most of the effort on the factors that will be critical: these will not all be known in advance. Moreover, the client company and its staff will often have already a great deal of knowledge of the field; and even though some of their information and opinions may be wrong, it is foolish not to take account of them as a starting point. For all these reasons a single preliminary briefing is quite insufficient and a study should usually be regarded as a joint effort with close continuing co-operation.

Where the company has a central economic, intelligence, or 'market research' department, it is often asked to undertake the commissioning of external studies on behalf of the operating divisions. This is excellent, in that it may provide a continuing liaison, as well as people who may view problems in the same way as the consultants. But there is sometimes a difficulty. It has unfortunately been found, even in large and highly-developed companies, that the economic or similar department is sometimes regarded as a group of 'back-room boys' who are asked for information but who hardly participate in its policy application. It may then happen that it receives a brief from operating division and is expected to 'place' this without any real access to the background which led to the request, the problems facing the division, or the ways in which the findings might be applied. When the firm's own economic department has this humble—and in this writer's opinion incorrect—role, the results may be worse than where the consultants are called in direct by the board or divisional management, when they are facing the decision-makers and can insist on a full presentation of the problem and its background, with direct liaison during the study.

Generally, each study is complete in itself, but in this consultancy it has been found that the most satisfactory results for both parties are obtained when there is continuity with a client and there is a succession of studies over time. There is a growth of confidence and knowledge of individuals, as well as of the company's activities and organisation, while the client can tell by previous experience what value he will get for his fee. 'Shopping around' among consultants is no doubt necessary when work is first commissioned, and perhaps sometimes to bring in new ideas, techniques or specialisations; but it can also be wasteful. The client's problem, if he puts the job out to tender, so to speak, is that he cannot specify the content of the final report in the way that can be done with an architect-designed new building or a machine with a guaranteed performance. Indeed an attempt to tie down all details of the study in advance not only fails to guarantee its quality but may result in the wrong work being done. With regular clients it is sometimes found best to agree the fee and content of a preliminary stage, which may perhaps amount to a quarter of the expected whole, and then after a first report to meet again and decide how much work and of what kind will be in the client's best interest: this procedure does not lend itself well to competitive tendering.

The best results, therefore, would seem to be obtained where a group has called in the same consultants for a succession of jobs, some related to each other and some not, in its various operating divisions. In some cases there may be an annual retainer, but it is not a necessary condition. Eventually, the client group may ask the consultants to advise on matters of central business strategy and resource allocation: correctly, any major development for a project in one division should be judged in the light of alternative opportunities elsewhere in the group. But generally a decision is taken in its own right, so to speak, as long as it meets certain criteria; questions of overall resource allocation and the differential growth of a group's activities or divisions do not yet seem to have been greatly systematised. Where a group has set up a special organisation under its main board to deal with these matters, it is the final level at which economic consultants may be able to help, and this will also indicate where they can most effectively be used on divisional studies.

Techniques and Problems

To deal adequately with techniques and methods would need a full paper, so only two points will be made here: about the role of techniques and about future uncertainty.

In many cases questions of technique are raised, as though having sufficient expertise in the techniques of economic or market research will in itself enable one to carry out the necessary task, but this may not be so. A competent economic consultancy should be fully conversant with all the available techniques, and with an intelligent staff trained in research methods this should not be difficult to achieve. But the crucial question usually is, not how sophisticated the techniques are, but whether they are being applied properly to the problem. They should be regarded primarily as tools, and the main question is to see that one is using the right tool for the job.

This is not only a matter of pressure from clients, some of whom like to be dazzled by science and to buy reports that look technically impressive. A consultancy should employ people of the highest intelligence, and such people become fascinated both by problems and techniques, which is good. But there is a danger that the fascination may lead to the building of an elaborate model, which has to be fed with great quantities of information laboriously collected in the field, but which is inherently incapable of solving the set of problems under consideration because it cannot take account of some of the factors, which may be crucial.

The consultancy under discussion tries to allow its members some time for 'playing' new technical ideas, and it has indeed made a number of innovations. Most of its work on advancing techniques, however, has come in the fields most nearly akin to the natural sciences rather than the social sciences or the business world. For example, fairly sophisticated work has been done on demographic projections, on regional and employment analyses, and on spatially-related input-output analysis: but this has mostly been in studies for the public sector.

In the business world as a whole, it seems that the most highly sophisticated techniques are most useful for the routine jobs, where there is a regular and large flow of data and where improvements for its analysis can be applied. As a whole, the more highly developed mathematical and statistical techniques improve the sort of routine work that was done by rule of thumb or rather naïve accounting methods in the past; whereas the most difficult problems are those in the fields where decisions

M

were made by 'hunch' in the past. It is in these fields that a wide range of techniques is required, but each in itself is not of the highest sophistication because of the considerable uncertainty in the data available for analysing problems that look into the future.

Lastly, there is the great question of how to deal with future uncertainty in forecasting, and hence in studies which will assist policy formation. Perhaps one should not touch on it unless one writes a paper as long as Elwyn Jones' and J. Morrell's excellent one (Forecasting and Business Policy, *Advancement of Science*, March, 1966). But it is so central to economic consultancy that a comment must be made. Clients prefer single-figure forecasts for their simplicity, though they know they are of spurious accuracy. Research workers prefer to omit altogether a quantitative estimate for a factor where there is great uncertainty, even though they know it may be important. Ideally, the solution would probably be to attach a probability scale to each forecast, showing the calculated likelihood of deviations of given amounts up and down from it; but usually one has not a basis for quantifying the probabilities. In practice, what one has to do is to work on the basis of a (rough and uncertain) sensitivity analysis. That is to say, one has to establish which of the factors will most affect the future situation if they vary from their anticipated figure, and then do most of the work on improving one's knowledge of these factors. Even so it may not be possible to quantify them satisfactorily, and one may have to forecast the end-result with a number of provisos: 'if this happens . . . that will follow'. All the alternatives could be immensely complex, but the guiding rule and acid test is the relevance to the possible choices of action open to the firm, and on this basis a simplification is usually possible.

12

The Business Economist and General Management

by CAMPBELL FRASER

Many people with an economics training have become general managers in industry. Sometimes the economics degree will have had an accountancy qualification attached to it, and often enough the man will think of himself as an accountant rather than as an economist. Almost certainly he will have progressed in his firm through the finance side. Sometimes the economics degree will have been quickly, and occasionally, gladly forgotten as the graduate became a trainee, moved on in time to production or sales, and then if his talents merited it, was made a general manager.

These are the lapsed economists, at least within the terms of reference of this book. Doubtless their academic discipline will influence their attitudes, their work, and perhaps their progress, but they are a different kind from the breed of economists who became increasingly evident in industry about fifteen years ago (the economist in government goes further back), and who have tried to apply the methods in which they are trained to business problems.

Over the years business economists have grown steadily in number and influence and, contrary to the views of the cynics, their even more rapid advance recently has not resulted from the need of industry to employ interpreters who are capable of communicating with other economists in the Civil Service, but from industry's recognition that they earn their keep.

However, very few of these economists have become line general managers, and the number moving directly from an

economics department to general management must be
negligible.

This is hardly surprising. General managers are mainly
chosen from the line functions, from those who are regarded as
the decision-takers, with a few exceptions gathered in from the
older staff functions like research just to show that there is no
intentional bias.

But an ambitious man should not be inhibited from becoming
a business economist on that account. The chances are that as
time goes by more and more of us will be 'staff' as the computer
takes over a large part of fact analysis (and, if we are honest
about it, a larger share of decision-taking). In these circumstance
the economist, whose work complements the computer, will
assume a fuller role in his firm's affairs, and he will naturally
find himself more eligible for general management, provided he
possesses other qualities which seem to characterise general
managers as a whole, or, perhaps more accurately, the successful
ones among them.

These qualities, in my observation, are vision, courage,
energy and acumen, and roughly in that order. Few general
managers will agree with the selection or the ranking but that
should not be unexpected from a group which is notoriously
individualistic. I would like to look at these qualities in a little
more detail, see to what extent the economist's training,
knowledge and interests contribute to them, and then, within the
limitations of one man's prejudices, indicate how economists fit
them.

First, vision. One of the jobs that has been thrust upon the
economist is reconnoitring the future. At one time many
business economists complained bitterly about the imposition
(older members of the B.E.G. will recall the debates on the
subject in the early 1950's), claiming that they were analysts
rather than soothsayers, and that their forecasts had no more
validity than anyone else's. One has only got to say that sort of
thing often enough to be believed.

However, most economists in business had enough gumption
recognize that in an era of fast-moving change, forecasting was
a job that had to be done, and their training was probably as
suitable a preparation for it as any other. So they got down to

the job of doing it, using increasingly accurate techniques as they understood the difficulties better. In the company for which I work they can claim a fine record of consistent success.

Penetrating the future realistically—what I mean by vision—is also the most important job that the general manager has to do. He will say, self-disparagingly, that it is the job he finds most difficult, the job he would most willingly allow the future to take care of. It does require a very real act of discipline to disengage oneself from the immediacies of today to consider the maybes of tomorrow.

In a firm the discipline is often achieved by institutional means. Companies which believe in influencing their environment as well as reacting to it, have introduced systematic planning which not only involves setting down targets, product by product, for capital expenditure, turnover, profits and the rest over a period of years, but equally important requires that the ways of achieving them are clearly set out.

This kind of business planning has as much in common with annual budgets as Cinerama has with silent pictures. It does, however, have a great deal in common with the work of the business economist. That in itself might not be sufficient reason for putting him in the general manager's chair, but at least he would feel at home with that significant part of the general manager's work which deals with the preparation of the business plan; of course he might feel somewhat less comfortable when it came to its implementation.

Needless to say, businesses are not run on or by statistics as yet; they are very much concerned with people. Most general managers when asked what their main job is will say 'dealing with people', or something like that, by which they mean hiring and keeping the right people, and preparing them for the right jobs in future.

This is the aspect of vision that general managers enjoy most. They take it for granted that they know people well, and often they do. On the other hand, economists don't have that reputation; being entranced by facts and figures they are not expected to be perceptive leaders.

In fact the ability to manage is very much an individual thing. Good leaders are to be found in the most unexpected places, even in the economics departments. But if the economist in general gives the wrong impression—'desiccated calculator'—he has only himself to blame.

Although his training makes abundantly clear the extent to which problems are hedged around with imponderables, he often argues as if psychological factors can be kept separate from the more important and more virtuous economic factors. The truth is that they affect each other and become an amalgam. The real manager uses his humanity to allow for the imponderables.

The second characteristic of the successful general manager is courage, and particularly the courage of decision taking.

Those of us who think nothing of having another pint of beer or choosing a place to go on holiday may find it difficult to imagine that there is anything notably demanding about decision taking. But, as we should be aware, there are decisions and decisions, and those that the general manager takes are surrounded by the tensions of complicated circumstances, often by the snare of urgency, and always by the certainty of far-reaching consequences. Taking the right decision time and time again—for that is the standard the general manager is set—requires a cool head and a strong stomach.

Some economists will doubt that proposition. They would opt for the keen mind. The facts, or enough of them, are known, and the solution is 'obvious' or 'determinate'. The experience of the general manager is that obvious solutions are hard to come by. Although the economist is quick to appreciate the nature of a problem he often confuses that with the act of deciding, and it has not been my experience of him that he finds the crunch of decision taking comes easy.

There is a nice contrast here between the certainty with which the economist can advise decision takers, and his own lack of certainty when he comes to take decisions himself. Presumably his training, with its emphasis on the complexity of economic problems, inhibits purposive decision taking.

Of one thing I am certain: general managers do have courage, although I have never heard one claiming it for himself. They prefer euphemisms like nous or dedication, excellent qualities but additional to the need for plain, old-fashioned guts. Let the business economist aspiring to general management take consolation from the fact that his success will not only concentrate the mind but also strengthen the stomach wonderfully.

The third quality is energy. There may be general managers who are mentally or physically lethargic, but one seldom comes across them. The common case is the man who steps off the Atlantic plane at 7.30 a.m. on a Saturday morning, has a wall built around his rose garden before lunch, plays a round of vigorously inaccurate golf in the afternoon, and then, as his wife will tell you, gets restless because he has so little to do.

It is sometimes suggested that the general manager has had hard work thrust upon him in the years of full employment. While others have worked less hard or with reduced responsibility, he has had to make up the difference. There is something in this in the sense that managers as a group (including entrepreneurs in small businesses) are far and away the most hard working section of the community today. In the particular case of the general manager, however, I would not want to argue the case that he has hard work thrust upon him. His gusto for work is almost certainly a sign that it comes naturally. In any event, the potential general manager should reckon to carry a heavy load.

There is a kind of energy, vitality, that is especially desirable in leadership. It has the merit, almost by itself, of inspiring enthusiasm in others, of keeping colleagues on their toes, of maintaining a positive attitude to work. It is often associated with that least appreciated of business virtues, sustained good humour. Vitality is a quality that is difficult to describe but is easy to recognise. Not all energetic general managers possess it, but a lot of them do.

How does the economist measure up to energy? What can be said fairly is that economists are not lazy. The majority of those that I have worked with have known how to bend their minds; I find that in their favour. On the other hand, they are not noticeably possessed of vitality.

Finally, there is the quality of acumen which, in this context, incorporates a number of things; the tendency to be a trader rather than an administrator; holding hard to mental quickness but being rather suspicious of intellectual profundity; concerned with business fact rather than general fact. If he were given to philosophising about himself—but he isn't—the general manager would pride himself on these qualities. As he should. Heaven help him if he forgets he is a trader.

At the same time, some part of acumen, as I have described it, is a narrowing quality when economic and social change are as swift as they are. It tends to concentrate attention on the immediate interests of the firm, neglecting longer-term external factors which may be of great importance to a company's future success.

What a nuisance that a man cannot manufacture a product efficiently, sell it hard against competition, and in the process make a profit, without having to bother about the balance of payments, or the sterling/dollar rate, or the regulator, or fringe benefits, or the whole airy galaxy of Government-inspired change. As a race general managers have not been quick to understand the influence that macro-economics can have on the progress of a business. They often admire the rough straight-forwardness of state-trading in other countries, but they have a decided concern about state interference in their own. The older among them yearn for the greater freedom of another period.

Yet the emerging generation of general managers—the business trainees after the war—have grown up with the fact that the State does play a role in the economy. They understand this as well as they understand free enterprise, even if they prefer free enterprise.

For their knowledge of the current politico-economic scene they have gained greatly from the business economist, who is very much their contemporary and whose world that is. It would be from him, too, they would recognise the difficulty of forecasting but that an orderly attempt at it is worth more than 'hunch'. He would probably have provided their first insight into marginal costing and would have suggested that pricing policy is not always a matter of matching competition, (although goodness knows, it often is). Discounted cash flow, with its emphasis on time and weighting is also likely to have come from the economist.

Business managers are much less likely to fear facts and are more willing to listen to new methods because of the economist

AND GENERAL MANAGEMENT   177

than they would have been without him. That is intended as a worthy compliment.

To sum up. The economist, at least in business, is brought up on vision; he is among the more energetic members of the community; he has not shown himself to be particularly strong in the courage of decision taking but, as a staff man, he may argue that decisions should be taken by others; he probably does not have the acumen of the average general manager but the chances are he has a broader and more profound outlook that goes to compensate for his deficiencies, although anyone who thinks that trading is sharp practice should not impale himself on general management. On the whole I would have thought that the business economist is ready material for general management.

At what stage in his career this should take place is more difficult to say. As things are now he would probably have to move into a line job in his early thirties.

Of course, the problem may be resolved in another way. If the present finance division incorporates the computer, the economics department, and corporate planning, the business economist will almost inevitably move towards the area of decision taking. There is no reason why an economist should not head up such a composite division, and there are many reasons why he should. It will not have escaped the notice of the more interested observers of the current business scene that the finance side of some large companies, whose activities extend well beyond accounting, is headed up by men whose suitability does not depend on an accountancy qualification. As likely as not they will be economists.

In the history of business, the economist's time span has been short, but his progress has been rapid, and his future beckons invitingly.

13

Economics in the Business Schools

by R. J. BALL

Introduction

It is natural that the business school teacher should view the teaching of economics within the context of a wider appreciation of its relations to other disciplines that are relevant to business decision-making than the teacher in the usual university department of economics. The professional is, of course, inclined to resist the notion that there is any difference in the basic ideas that one is seeking to impart in both business schools and departments of economics. In a significant sense this is true—and the London Business School has declined to institutionalise any such differences by using terms such as 'managerial economics' or 'business economics' in either labelling its courses or its faculty. Nevertheless it is proper to emphasise that in the business environment it is often the case that the order of priorities and interest in the economics field may differ from that of a straight economics department, and in the teaching context may demand a rather different pedagogic approach.

In this chapter I would like to attempt to do briefly three things: (a) consider the role of the business economist and the place of economics in the life of the manager, (b) review the development of the subject and its relation to curriculum design, (c) discuss some of the pedagogic implications of the foregoing.

Economics and Management

One is often asked to debate the question, 'can management be taught?' and long and protracted discussions take place anywhere between the learned journals and the correspondence columns of the press. I think that this is almost inevitable if the question is taken at its face value, and given the same logical status as a query as to whether it is possible to teach the differential calculus. I am not sure myself what the question means if one attempts to do this. The difficulty is that if the answer is 'no', it implies that managers either have nothing to learn or what we would like them to acquire in knowledge and skill cannot be taught. The relevant question is not whether management can be taught, but what if at all it is worth trying to teach managers. A sensible approach to the problem is therefore not to start out with an attempt to establish and teach a subject called 'management' but to begin from a study of the manager's job, of the problems with which he is faced, and to identify areas of study which may assist him in being more effective in dealing with these problems.

Effective managerial decision-making draws on knowledge and skills in a variety of dimensions. Some required skills are human and social in that we need to be able to deal with people not only as individuals but also as groups and an awareness of the way in which individuals and groups behave and respond to various kinds of stimuli is an important addition to the manager's tool kit. Decisions also often demand knowledge of the way in which accounting and statistical information is collected and interpreted which focuses on skill in handling data at the required level. Thus managerial decisions draw on tools and results from the behavioural sciences, economics, accounting, statistics and quantitative methods, which strategically may be applied in the unifying conceptual frameworks of marketing, production management, finance, personnel management and overall corporate planning and policy. The manager's job cannot be defined adequately on any one dimension—it is in one sense a synthesis or integration of the disciplines referred to, and it is the function of management education to establish the links between these disciplines and the decision making of the manager. In this kind of framework, the issue as to whether 'management' can or cannot be taught has little meaning. What has meaning is a discussion of what is helpful and relevant to the manager in these fields and whether what is taught makes him any more effective. To have meaning the issue must be debated at the specific rather than the general level.

What is the role of economics in this context? It used to be said that economics was the study of the allocation of scarce resources amongst competing uses. This is in fact too restrictive a description by far of what economists do, but it is an essential part of the function of the study of economics which is highly relevant to managerial decision making. The manager acquires and disposes of scarce resources, such as men, machines and money, in order to achieve objectives that may be defined in terms of sales, profit or any other objective to which the specific management may be geared. The manager allocates resources, from the scheduling of production with limited capacity on the factory floor, to the allocation of capital that emerges from the cash flow of a business or the money raised in the market. The study of economics is of major importance here in providing a conceptual framework with which to handle these problems, and in particular to establish criteria that define what, given the objectives of the manager of the enterprise, is an optimal allocation of the resources at his disposal. In this context an understanding of marginal analysis and the economists' view of cost is not only relevant but also in part a correction to the conceptual framework of the accountant which for one reason and another is not always satisfactory as a basis for rational decision making. The basic idea of economic optimisation not only directly relates to the decision making process, but also provides a conceptual framework within which to fit the technical approach to resource allocation of the operational research worker. Linear programming is nothing more than a mathematical application of basic economic principles.

The economist also supplies relevant information to the decision maker derived from a study of the way in which other decision makers, both consumers and producers, behave. Research into and study of the behaviour of such units contributes to planning and forecasting that is an integral part of the firm's operations. Here of course the degree of specialisation can be great and one does not expect that the general manager will himself be an expert in the field of, say, demand analysis. This is a job for a specialist in a staff function. Nevertheless, it is relevant and important for managers to have understanding of what is done in these areas in order that they may not only initiate relevant activities but be in some position to assess and discuss the status of results.

Finally, the economist is broadly concerned with the environment in which the firm operates. One definition of the specific role of top management is that it is concerned with the problem of relating the firm to that environment. In this context knowledge of how the economy as a whole is managed, how changes in the economy as a whole will affect the firm, is important from the point of view of policy making at the highest level. This is increasingly important in the U.K. economy, in view of the growing intervention of government in the business sector, and the impact of government on the out-turn of firms' decisions. For all these reasons the study of economics is a relevant activity for the developing manager.

The Development of Economics

Historically economics as a discipline emerged from what used to be called political economy. The great political economists of the eighteenth and nineteenth centuries such as Adam Smith, Ricardo and Karl Marx, were concerned very much with economic analysis in the setting of the economic system as a whole. They were very much concerned with the nature of the system and its future, and out of this grew concern for and interest in capitalism as a form of economic organisation or a variety of other socialist alternatives. What is to a large extent lacking in traditional political economy is a real concern for the micro aspects of the system as reflected in the decision problems and decision making processes of firms. Thus is was difficult if not impossible for the nineteenth-century entrepreneur to gain very much from the subject that he could relate explicitly to the kind of decisions that he had to take.

In a sense Alfred Marshall in the late nineteenth century was the founder of modern economics, not entirely in the originality of his conceptions, but in that for the first time a framework was developed in which the firm appeared as a decision making entity that in an integrated way was concerned with activities like production and pricing and the hiring and use of factors of production. This led to a sharpening and development of optimalisation criteria and these have to a large measure underpinned the structure of economic optimisation to this day.

There remained, however, two important problems. The first

is that while the development of criteria for optimal resource allocation in the firm began to emerge more clearly, the intellectual development that built on this foundation was still concerned primarily with an understanding of the workings of the economic system as a whole rather than with the problems of normative decision making as faced and judged by the firm. Economists were concerned more with what deduction could be drawn from the supposed behaviour of firms for the theory of markets and subsequently for general economic welfare. Political economy continued to rule. As late as 1965 a distinguished economist of the post-Marshall era, the late Sir Dennis Robertson, wrote: 'Economics is the study of man in the ordinary business of life or of the more material part of human welfare. It is a study worth pursuing partly for its intrinsic interest, but mainly because it may help us to form reasoned judgements on matters of public policy and pronounce on them as far as our opportunities offer.'* It is still true that the majority of degree courses in economics in this country point primarily to this end. The theory of the firm is not developed from the point of view of business decision making but as a foundation for discussing public policy with regard to regulating and controlling firms. This in itself indicates that a simple translation of conventional economics courses from university departments to the business schools is a doubtful proposition. One needs to re-think the use and inclusion of particular materials that are relevant to the objectives of management education. This does not exclude issues of public policy. Far from it for, as already pointed out, understanding of the environment and what affects it is essential to good business policy.

The second problem that was left was that the sharpened criteria for optimality developed by the neo-classical economists such as Marshall dazzled their progenitors into believing that their obvious rationality implied that such criteria were in fact applied by successful firms. At least at the static level, the optimal allocation of resources under perfect competition was established, and it was assumed that the forces of competition would themselves direct firms into realising the conditions laid down by the perfectly competitive theory. Departure from these

* *Lectures on Economic Principals*, The Fontana Library, 1965 p. 28.

conditions would result in inefficiencies, but while these might persist in the short run they would be eliminated by the long run forces of competition. The significance of this assumption was twofold. Firstly it suggested that the long run behaviour of firms and markets could be deduced from a small number of axioms related to profit and utility maximisation in markets. There was no need to conduct research into what firms actually did, it was implied, with the result that empirical inquiry took a back seat in the development of economics for several decades. Secondly, in the absence of empirical inquiry geared to sound analytical thinking, economics developed as a non-quantitative subject. As a result a long period elapsed before economists began the painful process of relating the conceptual framework of the discipline to the data of the real world. This demanded measurement which was singularly absent. The result of this at the level of the individual firm was the growth of the role, function and influence of the accountant in industry. The accountant was important because he measured. He possessed the mystique of number, and came to be the leading figure in pricing and investment decisions with which the economist is in theory so concerned with.

The pattern of course has changed and is changing. It is still however the case that many economics degrees are given with little or no attention paid to accounting or the use of statistical data and methods. In the business schools it is in the nature of things that the student will be exposed to both, and the teaching of economics can be integrated accordingly.

Curriculum and Teaching

The initial task facing the post-graduate student in the business school is an understanding of the basic principles of resource allocation. The first step is to develop for the student a conceptual framework for handling the internal and external problems of the firm. In the business school the purpose of the exercise is to assist in the development of effective managers and administrators, whether in public or private industry, in the sense of making 'better' decisions. In the context of the standard university department, little attention is generally paid to examining courses and course material against this criteria—or in some cases any real criteria at all. Liberal education tends to stand as its own justification. In the business school it is of major importance to establish the relevance of analysis and this is best done in practice by a constant attempt to relate the development of the field to the problem with which the manager will be faced. At the London Business School experiments are being carried out with the use of various sorts of case material which allow a constant dialogue to take place between the body of principles that are being laid down (e.g. with regard to resource allocation) and the embodiment of these principles in administrative situations. It is little good developing marginal analysis or incremental decision making concepts if the student is not given feed back from situations that enable him to identify the need to apply these principles in particular cases and have some idea of the practical difficulties that may emerge in application. In this context the case study has a number of advantages over the traditional essay. This approach means that teaching is more challenging both for the teacher and the student. It is aimed in part not only at 'teaching' the student but also at developing his own capacity to learn from his experience. Self-learning is as much an important part of the process as what is actually learned over a given period. It is challenging for the teacher for he is forced continually to review what is being done against the objectives of the course. The aim must be not to 'cover' conventional areas of economic thought but to equip the student to tackle economic problems that require a decision within the firm.

Given that this is so, the teacher of economic analysis and decision making in business schools faces another problem that traditionally falls outside the scope of the usual economics department, which is to place economic decision making in the environment in which it is carried out. This means that the application of economic principles has to be seen against (a) information systems that exist in firms including the role of the accountant and accounting data, and the staff economist and statistician, (b) the organisational framework in which decisions are made and the pressures that operate to modify decisions taken within that framework. If the economist knows nothing of this and cannot relate this to his own teaching which is thus put into perspective, the danger arises that all that results is a

N

compartmentalised body of knowledge, which the student is unable to relate to the world as he finds it as a manager. These problems are being recognised in the developments that are taking place in the modern theory of the firm. It is recognised that a positive theory of the firm must be rooted in some understanding of the decision making processes of firms which leads to an integrative approach that joins together economic analysis and the behavioural sciences. This view has implications for the academic organisation of business schools. In particular it argues against a rigid departmentalism which is a particular danger as the business schools grow. Few American schools have solved this problem adequately although many such as Carnegie recognise its importance and worry about it.

These problems are general to the activity of developing and applying economic analysis in business schools. In areas such as macro-economics, international trade and development, and the social control of industry, all of which contribute in an important way to the education of the manager, the divergence of objective and approach as against the typical economics department is less great, although the correspondence is not necessarily one to one. For example it is a valuable exercise to integrate the teaching of international trade and development with the problems of international business, more directly and immediately than might usually be the case.

The problem of teaching economics in the business schools presents an exacting challenge to those who believe that a sound foundation in the theory and practice of economics is a major contribution to effective management. It demands a degree of flexibility in approach and outlook that cuts across traditional academic departmentalism. It forces the economist to try and think clearly about the relation of his discipline to applied decision making. One's aspiration level must be higher than a desire to enable people to become intelligent readers of the *Economist* or the *Financial Times*. It focusses attention on the extent to which economic analysis contributes beyond the issues of public policy to the normative needs of the individual firm. In this area there is much that is challenging to the professional economist who is concerned to establish that he is teaching a professional subject.

14

The Business Economist:
An Appraisal

by T. M. RYBCZYNSKI

It is now more than 150 years since Burke wrote that famous and (by economists) often quoted sentence 'The age of chivalry has gone, that of sophisters, economists and calculators has succeeded'. Prescient though it was—or rather that part which related to economists—it is only in the last decade or so that it can be said to have come true.

Prior to the fifties, with the exception of the war period when together with a number of other specialists they invaded government on a large scale, economists were found predominantly in the world of learning. There were some in government, some acting as advisers to financial, industrial and other organisations, and some in journalism. Their numbers, however, were very small and to a large extent their functions were those of administrators or executives who used their economic expertise together with other skills. As a separate profession, that is to say, using their economic training in the way doctors, accountants and lawyers do, economists were virtually non-existent.

It was only some ten years after the war that the new profession began to appear in strength outside the Universities. It was then that the term business economist was first coined emphasising the distinction between those engaged primarily in teaching, that is to say academic economists, those applying the art and science of economics to the broad policy issues facing the government without being directly concerned in their solution, i.e. political economists and those practising within the framework of business viz. business economists.

The growth of business economists in the early fifties was not a sudden phenomenon. It was rather a gradual process of gaining recognition and influence. There was no single cause responsible for this development. Wartime experience, which proved that they could be very valuable in day to day operations, the increasing number of economic graduates turned out by Universities and eager to apply their knowledge, and the example of the American companies and their affiliates in the U.K. setting up new economic departments and/or expanding their size, were no doubt important contributory factors. But there were also other more fundamental forces at work exerting their influence slowly but nevertheless powerfully. Among them the growth in the size of the business firm and its rapidly increasing complexity, steady expansion in the role of government and the all-pervading nature of its activities and growing pre-occupation with the future were probably the most important. The ability of economists to understand these forces, to interpret them and foresee their implications was instrumental in providing the stimulus to the growth of the new profession. In a way this development can be looked upon as the natural result of the improvement in knowledge, and resulting specialisation leading to the emergence and growth of new professions, of which that of business economist is but one.

The progress of the new profession of business economist began to gather momentum in the late fifties and the pace accelerated in the sixties. There are signs that the upward trend is even faster at present and that it is likely to continue undiminished in the years ahead.

Until the early sixties the spread of the new profession was confined principally to business proper, i.e. to profit making organisations. An increasing number of industrial, commercial and financial firms were setting up new economic departments, increasing the size of the existing ones and employing economists in special divisions and departments. This development had also been accompanied by the growth of independent economic consultancy firms, the emergence of economic divisions in management consultancy businesses and the increasing use made of the economist in the world of journalism, advertising and associated areas.

In the government service it was not until 1964 or so that the economic profession made a big leap forward. It was then that, as Anthony Sampson in his *Anatomy of Britain* has put it, 'the economists suddenly and determinedly entered their kingdom in Whitehall, flocking in almost as thickly as during the War'. Since that time they have become part and parcel of the central government and local authorities appear now to be following suit.

Unlike the U.S.A. there are no comprehensive statistics at present showing the number of economists outside the Universities, or the industries in which they work. The difficulty emerging clearly from the individual contributions in this book is that unlike any of the recognised professions, such as accountancy and law which have their own examinations and indeed the right of restricting employment to the members of the professional bodies, economists perform many varied functions which have been changing and are continuing to change very rapidly.

Such estimates as can be made suggest that at present there are some 1,400 economists in the private sector of the economy, including nationalised industries, and that the government and local authorities employ another 200 or so. Compared with the U.S.A. where according to the survey carried out by the American Economic Association there were in 1964 some 9,000 economists outside the universities, employed equally by government and business, the number of economists in the U.K. is relatively small, though there is reason to believe that the disparity is now disappearing.

Economists in the U.K. private sector comprise those working in industrial, commercial and financial firms, those who are independent consultants and those employed by special research organisations, trade unions and trade associations, as well as journalist and independent commentators. Industrial and commercial undertakings, particularly the large firms are the most important employers accounting for some 600 to 800. The financial world is only a little less significant, the numbers working in it amounting to some 300 to 400, of which a substantial proportion works in a field closely connected with financial investments and above all investment analysis. Other organisations, that is research bodies, etc., including independent

consultants and economic journalists account for the remaining
200 to 300.

The common and outstanding feature of the function the
economists perform in all these organisations as well as in government service is that they are basically of an advisory character,
that is to say they are staff functions as distinct from executive
or line responsibilities. What all economists essentially do is provide an assessment of alternative courses of action, to help
decision-makers to make a proper choice. The evaluation they
offer is made either with reference to special areas of activity or
the general policy of the firm and is either connected with external conditions and the bearing these have or the internal reper-
cussions that are likely to follow.

It is perhaps worth emphasising at this point that many members of the economic profession are primarily executives and
administrators whose principal task is that of taking decisions
which affect directly the present or future position of the organisation they work for. They find their economic training most
helpful and useful in discharge of these functions but having
reached that position they can be said to be economic practitioners only to a limited extent, a position not dissimilar from
that of many other professional men such as chemists, engineers,
etc., who in the course of their careers move away from their
original tasks to those involving policy making and policy execution. The function that practising economists perform has been
changing very rapidly in the last fifteen years or so but the broad
outline of their role is now becoming more clear. Originally the
main preoccupation of the practising economists was the interpretation of the events in the outside world and their bearing on
the affairs of organisations for which they worked. This task,
however, was not well defined and not easy to discharge. The
difficulties they faced have been best summed up by Lord (then
Mr.) Keynes who in his introduction to the Cambridge Economic Handbooks wrote, 'The theory of economics does not fur-
nish a body of settled conclusions immediately applicable to
policy. It is a method rather than a doctrine, an apparatus of
mind, a technique of thinking which helps its possessor to draw
correct conclusions.'

While this dictum still holds true the developments in the last twenty years in the field of theory and the much greater availability of statistical data and other information have now enabled economists to offer much more precise views supported by quantitative evaluation of the implications and consequences of changes in external conditions and internal actions.

As shown by the individual contributions to this book the three main areas in business proper where economists tend to be employed at present comprise general economic work, sales and market research and the financial sphere. Economists carrying out general economic work are mainly concerned with an accurate assessment of the external environment in which their firms operate, forecasting the future, dealing with the collection, provision and interpretation of a variety of information needed for management purposes and acting as a link with the outside world. Those occupied in sales and market research have as their main task the assessment of future sales and their potential. Finally the interest of those in the financial field covers the problems of capital and monetary flows, defined in the widest sense of this term.

The distinguishing features of their work are a preoccupation with the future and rapidly increasing specialisation. Forward assessment involving quantitative estimates is the basis of most of their work. It involves forecasts of the world and the U.K. economy, economies of other countries, and of particular industries and commodities of direct significance to the companies they work for. Specialisation is now extending rapidly in each of the areas mentioned. In the field of general economic work it involves concentration on short-term forecasting, long-term forecasting, commodity and industry forecasting. In the sales and market research areas it covers specialisation in specific commodities, while in the financial sphere it comprises project evaluation and financial analysis.

All these functions require first-class ability to use the apparatus of economic analysis, and also mastery of increasingly sophisticated and complex statistical techniques for special tasks.

These developments have been intimately associated with the growing complexity of business and can be expected to accentuate in the future. Of great significance in this connection has been the increasing tendency for more detailed description of the functions economists are expected to discharge on the one side and much clearer definition of their role and place within the firm. The spread of planning departments, closely linked with the financial department, specifically charged with the task of producing forecasts that are used as the basis of plans, financial, sales and others, both long-term and short-term is an outstanding reflection of the trend which still appears to be gathering momentum.

It is as a member of a specialised profession possessing mastery of a certain body of knowledge and techniques that can now be brought to bear directly on the affairs of the firm that economists are nowadays employed. The career path offered to them and opportunities available are as shown by the results of the survey, to be promising and compare well with those in other professions. In addition to advancing as a member of the profession business economists, as other specialists, have an opportunity of moving toward general management or executive duties. In many ways their training and experience makes them particularly well suited to taking policy decisions requiring first-class knowledge of the internal working of the firm and its relationship to the external world. This is now being recognised by the employing organisations though perhaps not yet as fully as it deserves to be, so that economists now move from specialised functions to those of a managerial character even within one of the stages of their careers.

The process of professionalisation now taking place raises a number of important problems of which those concerning the organisation of the profession, the relationship with other professional bodies and the universities are most important.

At the present time there is only one organisation, the Business Economists' Group, which caters explicitly for the needs of the practising economist. Though well established—it has been in existence for some fifteen years—its membership covers only about a quarter of their number. The Group has been very active in trying to ensure that its members have the necessary training and experience, that they are aware of the developments in the world of learning of interest to them, and that their position and status are recognised. Unlike the older professions, such as accountants, the Group at present holds no examinations for its members, insisting on a university degree for the basic qualification, and also a minimum period of experience.

The rapid increase in the number of practising economists, however, requires that they should be members of an organised body serving their interests. In the world of increasing specialisation and growing professionalisation, specialists in various skills sooner or later must join an organisation to ensure that members of the profession have the necessary qualifications, maintain links with the outside world, and above all with the world of teaching.

The practising economists have started tackling these problems, and have been successful to a considerable degree in solving them. Yet the pace of progress has been so rapid that even more effort is required, and only a distinctive grouping is capable of organising and directing such effort.

Notes on Contributors

K. J. W. ALEXANDER

Professor Alexander taught at the Universities of Leeds, Sheffield and Aberdeen before becoming Head of the Department of Economics at the University of Strathclyde in 1963. He has published articles on the theory of the firm, wage theory, trade union organisation, labour mobility, regional economics and other topics. He has acted as economic consultant to the Clyde Port Authority and is a Director of Fairfields (Glasgow) Limited.

A. G. KEMP

Alexander Kemp was educated at Aberdeen University 1958–62 where he was awarded the degree in Economic Science. Economist with Shell International Petroleum Company, London, 1962–64. Assistant Lecturer and Lecturer in Economics at University of Strathclyde 1964–65. Lecturer in Political Economy, University of Aberdeen 1966–. Main interests in Economics: Public Finance and the Economics of Developing Countries.

T. M. RYBCZYNSKI

T. M. Rybczynski is an economist working with one of the London merchant banks. A graduate of London University, holding B.Com. degree and the M.Sc.(Econ.) degree, obtained at London School of Economics. He has spent nearly twenty years in the City of London.

He has contributed a number of articles to a variety of journals, academic and others, dealing with international trade, finance and other subjects.

He has been the Chairman of the Business Economists' Group since 1963 and is interested in problems of industry, finance and international economic relations.

C. ROBINSON

Colin Robinson is 34 and was educated at Stretford Grammar School (Lancashire) and Manchester University, where he graduated

B.A.(Econ.) 1957 with First Class Honours, and was awarded the Gladstone Memorial Prize. From 1957 to 1960 worked for Thomas Hedley and Co. Ltd. (now Procter and Gamble) as economist. Joined Esso Petroleum Co. Ltd., in July 1960 and worked until recently in Corporate Planning Department as economist. Appointed Head of General Economics and Energy Division of that Department mid-1965. Now Economics and Planning Adviser in U.K. Natural Gas Office of Esso Europe Inc.

J. A. CLAY

J. A. Clay read P.P.E. at Oxford before the war and then became articled to Price Waterhouse. This training was interrupted by War Service and he qualified as a Chartered Accountant in 1947. In 1948 he became personal economic assistant to the Finance Director of the Ford Motor Co. Ltd. In 1952 he went as economist to Tootal Broadhurst Lee Co., the textile group in Manchester, and in 1956 he became economic adviser to the Rio Tinto Co. Ltd., which subsequently became the Rio Tinto-Zinc Corp. Ltd., where he has been ever since.

Interests have been in the economic situation and prospects of the U.K. and overseas countries where his employers were operating or selling; secondly the international markets, e.g. textile fibres and non-ferrous metals with which the Company was concerned, and thirdly various industrial problems within these industries. He has published various articles in the press and in bank reviews.

More recently, involved in problems of overseas investment and concerned with the interim report by Mr. W. B. Reddaway on this subject which was commissioned by the C.B.I. Has also visited and written economic reports on Japan, Rhodesia, Australia and Canada, and is concerned with international bodies dealing with copper, lead and zinc.

G. BANNOCK

Graham Bannock is Company Economist and Chief of Market Research at the Rover Company Ltd. He graduated from the London School of Economics in 1955 and after military service in France held positions in Economics and Market Research Departments of Ford, the Economist Intelligence Unit, and Richard Thomas and Baldwins Ltd. He first joined the Rover Company in 1958 and rejoined in 1962 after spending two years in the Economics Division of the O.E.C.D. Joint author with A. J. Merrett of *Business Economics and Statistics* he has contributed a number of articles to learned journals and other publications.

A. SYKES

Allen Sykes graduated B.Sc.(Econ.) from London School of Economics. Between 1955–60 he was in the Economics and Statistics Department of Unilever Limited, specialising in management accounting and business economics, financial planning, takeovers and capital projects analysis, and internal management consulting work. From 1960 to date he has been with Rio Tinto-Zinc Corporation Limited (international mining and industrial group). Head of Financial Section, Group Planning Department, and a director of RTZ Consultants Limited. His main work involves the investigation and optimisation of all substantial capital projects, including optimum financing, plus general planning work and negotiations. R.T.Z. Consultants is owned by RTZ and carries out considerable work for non-RTZ companies.

He has written in conjunction with Professor A. J. Merrett, including numerous articles on finance, capital budgeting, nationalised industries, insurance and consumer finance, etc., plus three books— *Finance and Analysis of Capital Projects* (1963), *Housing Finance and Development* (1965) and *Capital Budgeting and Company Finance* (1966).

J. DE SOMOGYI

Jan de Somogyi has been the head of Economic Information Department, Marks and Spencer, since 1958. He graduated in commerce at the London University in 1949 and for some years studied Business Administration as a part-time, post-graduate, student at the London School of Economics. From 1949 to 1955 he was with the British Transport Commission, first with the Chief Financial Officer of the Docks and Inland Waterways Executive, and then with the Statistics Division of the Commission's Finance Department, as economist-statistician. In 1955 he joined Marks and Spencer. An Associate of the Institute of Statisticians, Fellow of the Royal Statistical Society, member of the Business Economists' Group and of several informal discussion groups. He is serving on the Statistical Sub-Committee of the Economic Development Council for the Distributive Trades. He has lectured on problems of distribution, marketing and retail statistics.

P. J. CROPPER

P. J. Cropper (born 1927) took a degree in Political Economy at Cambridge in 1951 and was a member of the Political Economy Club, which at that time met in the rooms of Professor D. H. Robertson. On leaving university he spent two years in the finance and economics section of the Conservative Research Department and a year helping to set up a shipping statistical service. He moved to the City in 1954 to work as an investment analyst in a stockbroking firm and after three years on research switched to the institutional side of active stockbroking, in due course becoming a partner. In 1966 he crossed over from broking to investing and became a director of Portfolio Management Limited, a leading firm of City investment consultants. He was on the committee of the Business Economists' Group from 1963 to 1965, and has also been active in the Society of Investment Analysts, where he took particular responsibility for a study on Terminology launched by the European Federation of Financial Analysts Societies.

R. TURVEY

Ralph Turvey is a full-time member of the National Board for Prices and Incomes. Until August 1967 he was chief economist with the Electricity Council, London and was formerly Reader in Economics at the London School of Economics. He has taught at a number of American Universities and spent two years in the economic section of the Treasury. He has published two books, *The Economics of Real Property* and *Interest Rates and Asset Prices* and is co-author with George Break of a study of Greek taxation. He has also published a number of papers on a variety of topics including welfare economics and cost benefit analysis.

W. F. LUTTRELL

After graduating from Oxford W. F. Luttrell worked for the Shell Group on distribution and marketing, then with an engineering group on production. He returned to university to take a degree at the London School of Economics, followed by several years at the National Institute of Economic and Social Research. In 1959 he was a co-founder of Economic Consultants Limited, of which he is now chairman.

His publications include a two-volume study *Factory Location and Industrial Movement* (National Institute of Economic and Social Research, 1962) and numerous papers on subjects which include problems of interplant costing; industrial market research; the role of industrial holding companies; energy forecasting; regional development; industrial location and employment; urban transport; economic research and marketing strategy.

C. FRASER

Campbell Fraser has been Dunlop's Managing Director in New Zealand since early in 1967. Before that he was Marketing Controller at the Group Headquarters in London, with particular responsibility for publicity, economics, and market research. Fraser started his career as an economist with the Raw Cotton Commission in Liverpool, moving from there to the Economist Intelligence Unit, in charge of Industrial Research. In the early 1950's he was one of the small group who started the B.E.G. and was its first Chairman.

R. J. BALL

Professor Ball was educated at Queens College, Oxford, where he obtained a first class honours degree in Philosophy, Politics and Economics in 1957. From 1957 to 1958 he was Research Officer at the Institute of Statistics, University of Oxford; from 1958 to 1960 he was University Lecturer at the Wharton School of Business, University of Pennsylvania (U.S.A.). In 1960 he was appointed Lecturer, subsequently being promoted to Senior Lecturer, in the Department of Economics in the University of Manchester. He took up his appointment as Professor of Economics at the London Graduate School of Business Studies in October, 1965. Professor Ball is the author of *An Econometric Model of the United Kingdom* (with Klein, Hazlewood and Vandome), 1961, and of *Inflation and the Theory of Money*, 1964, as well as of a large number of articles on related subjects. He is also an economic consultant to Government and industry.